£2.

R2

Happy Christmas

Andy & Kaye Br

DAD

The Thrill of The Chase

The Thrill of The Chase

Celebrating
Hunting with Harrier Hounds
in New Zealand

Sarah Milne

Photography: Rob Tucker

TANDEM PRESS

TABLE OF CONTENTS

INTRODUCTION   Tally Ho! 8

CHAPTER ONE   Setting the Scene 16

CHAPTER TWO   A Guide to Watching Harrier Hounds Hunt 42

CHAPTER THREE   A Master's Day 62

CHAPTER FOUR   A Huntsman's Day 74

CHAPTER FIVE   A Master's View of a Hunting Year 88

CHAPTER SIX   A Huntsman's Year 98

CHAPTER SEVEN   A Day in the Life of a Whipper-in 114

CHAPTER EIGHT   Breeding a Pack of Hounds 122

CHAPTER NINE   Puppy Walking 130

CHAPTER TEN   Judging at Hound Shows 136

CHAPTER ELEVEN   Hunting Personalities 142

LOCATION OF NEW ZEALAND HUNTS

NORTHLAND

KAIPARA

WAITEMATA

PAKURANGA

ROTORUA–BAY OF PLENTY

MARAMARUA

EASTERN BAY OF PLENTY

WAIKATO

POVERTY BAY

KING COUNTRY

TAUPO

MAHIA

TARANAKI

EGMONT–WANGANUI

HAWKES BAY

RANGITIKEI

MANAWATU

DANNEVIRKE

WAIRARAPA

STARBOROUGH

BRACKENFIELD

CHRISTCHURCH

SOUTH CANTERBURY

WAIMATE

CENTRAL OTAGO

OTAGO

BIRCHWOOD

EASTERN SOUTHLAND

FOREWORD

THE GREAT THING ABOUT HUNTING in New Zealand is that it can be done on many different levels and for many different reasons. For hunting enthusiasts there is the fascination of watching a pack of hounds hard at work and, of course, the thrill of the chase and the excitement of crossing fantastic country at speed and the challenge of jumping whatever comes in front of you, whether it be a hunt rail, large hedge or even the famed full wire fence.

For many others, hunting in New Zealand can just be about having an enjoyable day out with friends, getting to ride over magnificent country with the most outstanding views and having the feeling of being close to nature and beast.

I love hunting for all these reasons and also for the fact that it now provides me with a non-competitive arena in which to follow my passion for riding horses. It gives me the greatest pleasure to come out on a very green young horse and then to end the day with the same animal who, in the space of a couple of hours, seems to have gained a year's experience. I can decide to be competitive and go to the front of the field or just relax, enjoy the companionship of friends and cruise along at the back.

My children now join me out hunting and it is one of the few sports that we can all participate in together as a family. To see the excitement on their faces and to watch their horsemanship skills develop is a joy to behold. And at the end of the day everyone can get together at the breakfast and recall the excitement of the hunt.

Sarah Milne and Rob Tucker have done a fantastic job of capturing the uniqueness of New Zealand hunting, and this book will bring joy to the heart of any hunting enthusiast from all parts of the globe.

Mark Todd

TALLY HO!

FIRST, TAKE ONE OF THE WORLD'S MOST BEAUTIFUL COUNTRIES. Include thousands of hectares of rolling countryside, interspersed with native bush, unpolluted waterways and sparkling lakes. Ensure there are backdrops of majestic mountains or kilometres of unspoilt beaches.

Next, add generous quantities of fun-loving people from diverse backgrounds, ages, occupations and socio-economic groups.

Throw in an equal quantity of bold jumping, free-moving horses, that are surefooted and courageous. Combine with hardworking, tenacious harrier hounds and an abundance of hares for quarry. Finally, garnish the ingredients with an equitable climate, realistic costs and accommodating landowners.

This is the recipe for hunting in New Zealand – an exciting sport in a very special country.

The Thrill of the Chase is a celebration of hunting with harrier hounds in New Zealand.

Equestrian journalist and hunting enthusiast Sarah Milne has combined with award-winning photographer Rob Tucker to create a book that captures the essence of this magical sport. There is an abundance of colour photographs, interviews with hunting personalities, plus a description of the various positions within the organisation of a Hunt.

Read, savour and enjoy!

A hunting day has this magic quality that transcends definition, that lifts us from the humdrum to the sublime and when the luminescence fades and we are left with the drab, some of the magic always lingers on.

Sir Patrick Eisdell Moore in *A Great Run*

Previous pages: Huntsman Steve Clark, with the Northland hounds, overlooking the Pacific Ocean, in the Bay of Islands during the Northland Hunt's Jubilee celebrations.

Left: Taupo Huntsman Harvey Wilson at the start of a hunting day at Western Bays, near Lake Taupo, in central North Island.

Following pages: Birchwood country, Southland, at the bottom west of the South Island. Huntsman Neil Hassall leads his hounds out at Wilanda Station, near Invercargill.

Left: The Central Otago countryside, invaded by hectares of flowering thyme, provides vast hunting possibilities for the local pack. Whipper-in and Central Otago President, Mac Wright, assists Huntsman Lloyd Brenssell.

Following pages: Waikato hounds, with Huntsman Lauryn Robertson, make their way along Te Akau Beach on the North Island's west coast.

Chapter One
Setting the Scene

FROM A HUNTING PERSPECTIVE New Zealand is a very young country. When the first recorded pack of harrier hounds in the world was established in the Penistone of Yorkshire in 1260, New Zealand was still undiscovered by Europeans. Abel Tasman first sighted New Zealand's mountainous, bush covered terrain three centuries later, but it wasn't until the 1870s that early European settlers set out to establish hunting in the young colony. This was no easy feat, as there was neither quarry to chase nor hounds to follow. But there were imported horses to ride and many hectares of cleared grassland interspersed with native bush and bounded by mountains and sea. The European settlers imported and naturalised hares, and even attempted to import a pair of breeding foxes — a venture which failed when the pair met a watery death at the bottom of Lyttelton harbour in 1876, courtesy of a vigilant customs officer. A ship's doctor imported the first harrier hounds and the first hunt to be formed was the Pakuranga Hunt in 1873, located near Auckland, now New Zealand's largest urban area.

Other hunts were established throughout the 1880s and beyond. Several early media reports mention brave and enthusiastic riders who were not always in complete control of their horses yet tackled the enclosures of hedges, rails and stone walls with bravado. No doubt it was this bravado that helped riders cope with jumping wire fences. In England it was regarded as a heinous crime for a hunting farmer to have wire on his property, but in New Zealand fencing methods changed throughout the late 1800s and wire became increasingly popular. Initially it was thought that it was impossible to jump wire, but in 1895 Colonel Charlton Dawson, the master of the Pakuranga Hunt, encouraged the initiative and it was soon reported that 'wire is now jumped as readily as any other sort of fence'.

In 1900, a governing body called the New Zealand Hunts' Association was formed from the

nine packs that were hunting regularly. The recorded history of these early hunts provides fascinating reading. There was terrific determination to keep the hunts alive, even when faced with a nationwide distemper epidemic, two world wars and the Great Depression during the 1930s. In true pioneering fashion, many hunt masters and other members dug deep into their own pockets to carry the hunts' financial affairs through periods of crises. Others kennelled and maintained packs at their own homes so that the hunts could continue.

Above: Riders depart from a paddock set aside for trucks at a Rotorua-Bay of Plenty meet.

Far left: Birchwood hounds in the tussock with Huntsman Neil Hassall.

A clean pair of heels over a Manawatu spar.

Over time enthusiastic people established more hunts, and today there are 28 with a total membership of over 4,400 people. The hunts range from profitable incorporations with investments in commercial property to small organisations run primarily by enthusiastic farmers who subsidise the keep of the hounds with their own money. Anyone prepared to abide by the rules and capable of paying a subscription can join. Hunting in New Zealand is a classless sport where people from a range of occupations, wealth, age and riding ability meet to enjoy an activity that is easy to access and, when compared to the United Kingdom, remarkably inexpensive. New Zealand's equable climate allows the horses to live outdoors all year, which means they are cheaper to keep, and subscriptions average around $200 (£70) for the season. Each hunt organises its own social and fundraising activities. These may include summer treks, raffles, balls, dances, cattle-raising schemes, hound auctions and hunter trials. Several hunts were entitled to hold public race meetings, but these are no longer popular as changing policy on the distribution of totalisator profits has curtailed the profits.

Throughout the two main islands that make up New Zealand the topography varies markedly. In the South Island regions of Otago and Southland there are big open spaces covered in native tussock with breathtaking backdrops of snow-covered mountains and alpine lakes. Further north, the Canterbury region has kilometres of flat arable plains where the paddocks are often divided by large gorse hedges that invite fast, bold jumping. On the east coast of the North Island, the hunting country is steeper and often interspersed with native bush and streams, demanding hardiness and stamina from both horses and riders. In other North Island areas, particularly on the west coast and around the urban centres of Hamilton and Auckland, the land is fertile and undulating and is farmed more intensively, resulting in smaller paddocks that ensure many jumping opportunities.

The field watches with anticipation as Taupo hounds put up a hare at the start of the day, and commence a huge run up a steep hill.

At the Northland Hunt 50th Jubilee – far left: Kaipara Master Inga Knier, left: Past Kaipara Master Jo Hall, below: Judy Hall of Waikato Hunt.

The scenery is equally as diverse as the terrain. New Zealand is probably the only country in the world where the same pack of hounds in a single month are able to hunt alongside boiling geothermal geysers and sulphur lakes, close to commercial ski fields, and beside scenic volcanic lakes.

Although the components of hounds, countryside and scent are common to the sport, some of the fundamental parts of a hunting day that New Zealand riders take for granted differ from the English or American foxhunting experience. One of the main differences is the jumping of wire. Most New Zealand hunt fences involve wire in some form. The majority of paddocks are enclosed by post and wire fences around 1.10–1.15 metres high. Some hunts lower the top wire in places, and rails may be added to make the jumps more inviting. However, some properties have no such preparation, and horses and riders simply negotiate the full fences. Although many visitors to New Zealand are initially shocked by the idea of jumping wire, most horses clear the fences with ease and the riders' confidence quickly grows. There are certain advantages in jumping wire fences, as the height and width never vary and it is always possible to see what lies on the far side. Some farms have barberry, boxthorn or gorse hedges, and there are occasionally post and rails, ditches or cross country fences to negotiate.

At a typical New Zealand hunt meet there is plenty of parking in a field, and people normally transport their horses in lorries or trailers. Hounds usually move off at midday, and the hunting day lasts between two-and-a-half and four-and-a-half hours. Riders then wash their horses, feed them and leave them tied to their lorries or trailers while they attend the hunt 'breakfast'. This is

a New Zealand hunting tradition where everyone gathers together, often in a woolshed or implement garage, to socialise and enjoy food contributed by the riders. Invariably there is a hubbub of hunting gossip, shared stories and laughter. Landowners are encouraged to attend and the master will make a speech to thank them for their generosity in allowing the hunt to cross their land. Sometimes the hunt breakfast overflows into a spontaneous evening of fun and music, dancing and partying – but not before the horses have been bedded down for the night.

The horses and ponies used for hunting vary in type and size. Retired racehorses sometimes find a new career on the hunting field, and crossbred hacks are also popular. Some riders use their horses for show jumping, eventing and dressage activities during the summer months, then take them hunting in the wintertime. Many good competition horses have started their careers in the hunting field and New Zealand event riders Mark Todd, Blyth Tait, Andrew Nicholson and Vaughn Jeffries have all enjoyed the sport. Mark Todd is now a familiar sight in the Waikato Hunt, enticed back to the sport by the enthusiasm of his children Lauren and James.

In New Zealand it is unusual for horses on the hunting field to be plaited, and some have long manes and tails. Others may have hogged manes. Regardless of the horses' turnout, members are expected to wear correct hunt attire. When invited they can wear their hunt's uniform, which

Above: King Country Hunt is a small hunt in the central North Island where the 42 members work together with tenacity to fundraise and finance their sport.
From left to right are: Joint-Master Lance Neeley, Immediate Past-Master Jon Nelson, Huntsman Phil Havord, Joint-Master Malcolm Wills and President Barry Stott.

Hunters waiting to be saddled.

Camaraderie and fun — what better way to spend a day?

includes a coat in a specific colour with the hunt colours on the collar. Riding hats are compulsory, and some hunts insist on safety hats.

The hunting season starts at the beginning of autumn, around late March or early April, when Northern Hemisphere enthusiasts are hanging up their boots and spurs for the season. Temperatures in New Zealand can still be quite warm at this time of the year, often in the mid-twenties, which can provide challenging scenting conditions for the hounds and a heated day for the field in their traditional winter coats and black boots. Mid-winter temperatures are cooler — three to fifteen degrees centigrade being the norm — and the occasional South Island hunt may encounter snow. A hunting day is rarely cancelled, and this generally occurs only when ground conditions are very wet.

Each hunt employs a huntsman* to care for and hunt the hounds. The salary and conditions differ between the hunts. Some of the smaller rural-based hunts rely on their members to look after the hounds during the summer months, and the huntsman is only employed on a seasonal basis from February to July. Other hunts are larger, more financial and can afford to own properties on which the huntsman is based throughout the year. Huntsmen are responsible for supplying their own horses and equipment. On a hunting day enthusiastic amateur whippers-in assist them.

Traditionally hunting in New Zealand is a highly social activity both on and off the field. There is a special camaraderie among hunting friends. Lasting friendships are formed, based on a mutual love of a sport that combines speed, adrenaline, risk and pleasure. Many people hunt as family groups, with sometimes as many as three generations enjoying the sport together.

Overall, hunting with harrier hounds in New Zealand is in strong heart. It attracts a group of enthusiastic followers, and the sport is accepted as an integral part of the rural environment. Riders who enjoy hunting are friendly and hospitable, and the common elements of horses, hounds and countryside make for an enduring comradeship.

Following pages: So many different types of horses yet all with one intent — to gallop and jump and follow the chase. Riders and horses wait during a check at Te Akau.

Pages 28,29: Northland Master Colin Finlayson leads a big field of over 300 riders during Northland Hunt's Jubilee celebrations in the Bay of Islands.

* Huntsmen are usually men, though there have been some notable exceptions. However the term used is still 'huntsmen'.

  Currently, of the 28 'huntsmen' in New Zealand, there are no women.

Hunting is a sport, pure and simple, and must be one of the very few such sports left.
There are no international visits, no Olympic representation, no sponsors to be sought,
no trophies to be won — the only rewards are the thrill of the chase, the joy of a good horse
under, and the satisfaction of watching and understanding hounds at work.

Len McClelland in *The Horse in New Zealand*

Following pages: Starborough Hunt, founded in 1947, is a family-oriented amateur hunt. Lyell McLauchlan has kennelled the hounds and been Master since the beginning, and Peter Vavasour is an amateur-huntsman with passion and professionalism. Here, the small mid-week field wind their way along some steeper Marlborough country in the northern part of the South Island, while the hounds cast with unrelenting energy.

Above left: Manawatu Master Mark Goodwin, and Hawke's Bay Huntsman Murray Thompson.

Right: On a roll. Rotorua-Bay of Plenty riders negotiate a spar built from battens and black plastic poly-pipe.

Above left: Over the full wire fence, complete with barbed-wire outrigger, at Christchurch Hunt's closing meet.

Below left: Fence battens can be either wooden or metal, as the South Canterbury fence at left shows. Regardless, the obstacle is there to be jumped, as this rider demonstrates mid-run at the closing meet.

Right: On a run at South Canterbury's closing meet.

Pakuranga Huntsman Ross Coles leads the field
home after an autumn day's sport at Port Waikato.

Above: Taranaki members socialise while their horses enjoy a welcome drink on an autumn day at Croydon Road in East Taranaki.

Right: Sarah Milne hoses down a hunter after a warm afternoon meet.

Above left: Relaxing in the truck park after a Northland Jubilee meet.

Above and right: Northland Hunt Jubilee breakfast in a woolshed.

The Hunt Ball is one of the highlights of the hunt season. It is usually held in mid-winter and features a live band, dancing and an extensive buffet meal. Pakuranga Hunt's ball in 2003 had a masquerade theme.

Far left: Sherri McTaggert and Sue Fuller.

Left: Hess Hargraves, here with wife Heather, took the prize for the best costume.

Right: (left to right) Mark Chrisp, Julie Evans, Simon Bennett and Sarah Milne.

Far right: Simon Bennett, Grant Schultz, Simon Eisdell Moore and Pakuranga Master Ivan Bridge.

CHAPTER TWO

A GUIDE TO WATCHING HARRIER HOUNDS HUNT

WITH HUNTSMAN ROSS COLES OF THE PAKURANGA HUNT

ONE OF THE SIMPLEST PLEASURES of hunting is watching hounds work. There is incredible energy in a well-matched pack of hounds as their instinct drives them to pursue the scent of a hare. During the hunting day the hounds will face many different challenges, and many people find the more they understand of these aspects, the more they enjoy watching the hounds.

Ross Coles is a huntsman with a lifetime of experience. He is an ideal person to explain what happens during a hunting day. His father, Ray, was huntsman for the Pakuranga Hunt for 28 years and Ross helped as whipper-in from an early age. Ross took over after Ray retired in 1982, and he is now one of the longest serving huntsmen in New Zealand. His involvement with racing, as clerk of the course at the frequently televised Ellerslie race meetings, makes Ross one of the most recognised huntsmen. He has represented New Zealand in show jumping and has been both chef d'équipe and chef de mission for New Zealand equestrian teams to the Olympic Games and world championships.

The Pakuranga Hunt borders South Auckland, New Zealand's largest metropolitan area. The country includes a mix of dairy and sheep farms over undulating land divided by hedges and wire fences. Many hunt properties are adjacent to busy roads or urban developments, so it is essential for Ross and his whippers-in to maintain tight control over the hounds while still encouraging their independent hunting instincts.

Ross is proud of the hunting traditions and etiquette associated with the sport that has dominated his life. But he is also a realist and well aware of the demands of the riders in the field. 'When I am hunting I am always thinking about the field,' he says. 'On an average day 70 to 100 people hunt with Pakuranga and they all want to be entertained. Some have come to jump. Some have come to hunt. I want them all to go home having enjoyed their day. That makes me a huntsman

Pakuranga hounds await the hunt.

and an entertainer. I manage the sport within this consideration. For example, I want a pack of hounds that hunt, but are also a biddable pack so that if they run out of bounds I can stop them, bring them back, and they will immediately put their heads down and hunt again. The Pakuranga hunting environment is no place for the purist huntsman who won't lift* his hounds to get them back in bounds.'

At a meet Ross is the consummate professional, always immaculately turned out, well mounted and punctual. He delights in encouraging members to enjoy their sport and is always willing to answer questions about hunting. 'When the hounds come out of the truck [travelling pens] they are full of energy and ready to hunt,' explains Ross. 'However, the first task is for the two whippers-in to "pack" them up into a group so that they follow me to the country to be hunted. Once we arrive there, I encourage my hounds to "cast". This is when the hounds scatter round the paddock, out in front of my horse, searching for the scent of a hare. My aim is for the hounds to work thoroughly through each paddock.'

* The term 'lift' means the huntsman and the whippers-in influence the hounds to lift their noses from the ground and stop scenting until they have been moved to a different area. Then the hounds will be encouraged to start scenting again.

Above: Huntsman Lloyd Brenssell counts
the Central Otago hounds out of the truck.

Right: Pakuranga Huntsman Ross Coles.

Taupo Huntsman Harvey Wilson, the hounds and field of riders head home after a successful day's sport at Kuratau, Taupo.

Hounds hunt by smell, not by sight. During the day most hares squat in a grass field or in a crop, in a place called a 'form' or 'den'. The hounds will search for the 'line' of scent that the hare has left on the ground leading to their hiding place.

'I try to work through the boundary paddocks first so that if a hare is "put up" she will hopefully run into the country we can hunt,' continues Ross. 'It is frustrating to put up a hare in the middle of a small property and watch her run straight out of bounds.' For other huntsmen who have larger properties to hunt over this is not an important consideration. 'I try to work the low ground first, because hares tend to run up hill, so if the hounds put up a hare we can have a good run to the hillier areas.'

While the hounds are casting or working at a check the riders in the field will probably be relaxing, perhaps sipping from their hip flasks and chatting. But Ross remains completely focused,

watching his hounds and ready to move at any time. 'When the hounds are casting I look for signs that there is scent around. One of the best signs is when the hounds' sterns [tails] wag more frantically than usual. Often one hound will work a line and, without making any noise, other hounds will congregate. As they become more confident they will make noise, then all the hounds will move to the line. My hounds won't make any noise until they are confident.'

The hounds then start to follow the line of scent, gaining speed as they do so. The sight and sound of a pack in full flight is exhilarating. Ross will blow 'gone away' on his horn, as the riders in the field gather their reins, preparing to follow. 'When my hounds are running I like to be about 200 metres behind them. A huntsman should never lead his hounds. They need to be left to their natural instincts.

'While the hounds are running I am always listening. Hounds' voices tell me a lot of things. For

example, if they are pursuing a rabbit or possum in a bush their voices have a higher pitch. If they are running on a hare they make deeper, more melodious music. If they are close to the hare their voices sound more excited. If the hounds are running and they stop making noise it usually means the hare has turned or double-backed and the hounds have overrun the scent. They shouldn't over-run by more than 50 to 100 metres before stopping.' This is called a 'check'. Then, to try and find out where the hare has gone, the hounds need to 'wheel', which means they turn in an arc as they search for the scent.

'If the hounds can't find the scent they generally wheel wider,' continues Ross. 'Older hounds, in particular, will move further out. If they are unsuccessful by their own casting I will become involved and start from where they last gave noise. I will work a horse shoe shape from that point. If a hare has run far enough in front of the hounds she may have retraced her steps and then branched off, hence the reason for casting in widening circles. I will also ask myself: If I were a hare where would I have run? I look for a track, broken ground, perhaps a steep face, or a gully.

The quarry sprints away.

Hares don't usually run to water, they usually run around it. But they will often run up a hill. Hares have powerful hind legs, which they use to help them escape by speeding up hills.

'A hare will usually only run in her own territory. She does not live underground and she knows her territory intimately because it is her best means of survival, so she will use every trick possible to escape the hounds. Her tactics may include running on a tarsealed road or laneway, or swimming across a creek. In steeper country people have seen hares leap out from the side of a hill. All of these tactics put a break in the scenting pattern, which means the hounds have to work harder, and it slows them down. Occasionally a hare may hide underground, for example in a pipe, but it is rare. If she does, I won't dig her out.

'As a hare tires she becomes darker, runs in smaller circles and leaves less scent. This means it is more difficult for the hounds. Often a hare will make a break on the hounds and then a fresh hare will jump up in the near vicinity. In this situation it can be difficult to keep the hounds working on the line of the hunted hare. The purists say that you should keep pursuing the hunted hare, but this

Hunting is like a party on horseback.

Adrienne Taylor

means stopping the hounds from running on the fresh hare, lifting them and then trying to put them back on the scent of the original hare, which meanwhile has run further away. It is a challenging situation.

'For me hunting is not about killing. It is about the thrill of the chase. It is an adrenaline rush for most riders to gallop across country and jump the unexpected. The nearest thing to it is eventing, but in that sport the riders have walked the cross-country course before they jump it. When you go hunting with the Pakuranga Hunt you arrive on about 1,000 acres, maybe owned by 15 different farmers, and nobody knows where they will ride and what they are going to jump. The prepared fences are no lower then 90 centimetres and there may be some full wires to jump that are around 1.15 metres, depending on the terrain. Then there may be some hedges as high as 1.5 metres. There is usually a lot of jumping, maybe around 100 fences in one day, because many of the paddocks are so small.'

If there is a kill or the pursued hare escapes, Ross will move his hounds to fresh country and cast them again. The day is over when the master decides, usually after about three hours of hunting. Then the whippers-in pack the hounds up and they follow Ross back to the hunt truck.

The Pakuranga Hunt is one of the busiest in the country, with meets carded two or three times a week from mid-March through to late-July. Although the hunting environment has changed over time, with increasing subdivision shrinking many properties, Ross provides excellent sport. Doctor Ivan Bridge, Master of the Pakuranga Hunt, says, 'Our hunt is blessed with Ross. He is very much part of the team. He takes a pride in the hunt and he is professional in what he does. He works to provide the best sport possible for the field in the limitations of the country.'

For Ross the sport of hunting is an integral part of his life, and he is fortunate to be able to combine his sporting passion with his profession.

The Hawke's Bay hounds show unrelenting energy.

60

Above: Waikato hounds heading home with
Huntsman Lauryn Robertson at Arapuni.

Previous pages: South Canterbury
Huntsman Ryan Smith 'blowing to the kill.'

Right: Pakuranga's Royal.

Below left: Brackenfield hounds at the end of the day.

Below right: Pakuranga hounds enjoy a brief break.

Above: Homeward bound at Pio Pio in the King Country.

Above left: Pakuranga members Nicki Van der Brink
and Sue Fuller (top), Bridgette Fulton (centre),
Julie Evans (bottom).

CHAPTER THREE

A MASTER'S DAY

WITH MASTER HARVEY WILSON, OF EGMONT-WANGANUI HUNT

WITHIN EVERY HUNT THE MASTER'S ROLE is critical to the success of a day's hunting. The role is multifaceted and involves much more than the highly visual part of leading the field. The master has ultimate responsibility for the organisation of the day, including liaison with the property owners. He or she also has complete authority over the field. In addition, the master's style tends to be mirrored by the mounted followers. For example, a master who is able to gallop and jump with flair raises the standard of riding in the field, as members try to emulate the master's performance to keep up with the action. The best masters are invariably followed by inspired riders.

Harvey Wilson is one of New Zealand's longest serving and most popular masters. He has led the field at Egmont-Wanganui Hunt for seventeen years and his wife Ann and daughter Sarah hunt with him when they can. Hunting is not the only equestrian activity in the Wilson household as Ann and Harvey are New Zealand's most successful show jumping couple. Harvey has represented New Zealand on several occasions including a tour to the United Kingdom in 1976. On this trip he met Ann Fenwick, winner of the 1977 British Lady Rider Championship. Love blossomed and Harvey and Ann married in 1977. They have become a formidable team in New Zealand show jumping circles and their wins have included the Horse of the Year title on four different occasions. During the winter months when many show jumping riders rest after the relentless demands of the summer season, Harvey and Ann simply change their riding coats and go hunting.

Harvey has clear goals for his role as a master. 'I get my thrill out of seeing people enjoying themselves,' he says. 'If we are having a good run and I look round and see happy expressions on the faces of the people who are following, that's the thrill for me. We have some people who want to be up the front, some people who don't and some people who never jump a fence. It doesn't matter as long as they are enjoying themselves.'

Right: Harvey Wilson at Hurleyville, South Taranaki.

Harvey Wilson enjoys the hunt
breakfast at the Hurley family farm
at Hurleyville.

For Harvey, the role of master includes being well mounted. 'I believe that a hunt should never be inconvenienced by either the huntsman's or the master's horse. Being well mounted is important. Normally I will have a spare horse back in the field, or maybe if something went wrong with mine, I could swap with Ann.' Harvey's hunters are all well schooled and immaculate jumpers, and they are also beautifully turned out. 'I always make sure my hunters are plaited. I feel if the master doesn't lead the way with turnout then there is no standard to follow. James Cropp, our huntsman, is also always well turned out.'

Egmont-Wanganui Hunt is based on the west coast of the North Island among some of the most productive dairy farming country in the world. The fertile soils, temperate climate and

Master Harvey Wilson thanks the property owners at the hunt breakfast.

prolific rainfall produce an abundance of grass, which feeds a dairy industry that exports to world markets. The rolling countryside is dissected by big boxthorn hedges and overshadowed by the picturesque dormant volcano of Mount Taranaki in the north. Egmont-Wanganui Hunt, founded in 1894, is one of the oldest hunts in New Zealand.

Egmont-Wanganui members are proud of their master and prepared to voice their opinions. According to long-time member Michael Steele, 'Harvey makes our hunt. When there is no action he looks after the children and the not-so-able members. Then, when there is a run, he extends everyone!' Hunt President Peter Brosnahan agrees. 'Harvey is a complete horseman who has an intense love of hounds and understands the whole process of hunting. For Harvey, riding a horse

Above: Master Harvey Wilson discusses the hunting country with Huntsman James Cropp.

Right: Egmont-Wanganui members.
Top left: Sally Durr, top right: Michael Steele, Egmont-Wanganui Life member, bottom left: Emma Richardson, bottom right: Matthew Cropp.

is second nature so his dominant attention is focused on the hunting. In the seventeen years that Harvey has been master he has elevated the quality of horsemanship in the field. He makes it look so easy that he engenders confidence in those who follow him and this increases the joy of the sport for the field.'

On a hunting day Harvey aims to arrive about three-quarters of an hour before the hunt starts. 'I like to chat with the property owner and ensure everything has been attended to,' he explains. 'Then I throw off at the dot of twelve.

'We are a happy hunt and a lot of that comes from our Huntsman, James Cropp. James loves his hounds and they want to hunt for him. It can take James a long time to put his hounds away after a day's hunting because he wants to pat the good ones, and then he'll pat the bad ones too, just to reassure them and let them know he's confident that they'll do better next time. James has the same attitude if his horse ever stops. He'll never thrash his horse; he'll just turn it around and present it a second time. That good attitude spreads through the field.'

Egmont-Wanganui hunting country ranges from dairy pasture with boxthorn hedges, tape and rails to sheep country, which has more wire. 'It is well prepared,' says Harvey. 'But if we are running and I know the landowner is happy then we follow the hounds over whatever fences come our way.'

I enjoy the wonderful country we hunt over with its magnificent scenery, the great jumping, and the fact it is such easy footing for the horses after being brought up on the plough. There would be many people in England and all over the world who would give anything for a few days' sport with a good pack of New Zealand hounds.

Ann Wilson in *Gone Away, One hundred years with the Egmont-Wanganui Hunt Club*

The standard of jumping in the Egmont-Wanganui field is very good. 'We don't get too many breakages. If someone breaks an electric tape* we'll ask them to fix it so that usually deters people from jumping them unless they are confident they will clear them. I don't encourage people to do things that are beyond them. That's when people get hurt and things get broken. One exception was the day I led the field over a big, old, wooden boundary gate. After I jumped it, I yelled, "Be careful" in the hope that no one would follow. Of course they did, and in the process the gate was smashed to smithereens. The problem was no one was forthcoming about who did it.' Harvey found there was a 'code of silence' among the field and no one would own up to the breakage. 'I eventually found out that Ann was the culprit!' laughed Harvey.

When Harvey is hunting he is keen to watch hounds work and tries to position the field in the best vantage points. This is an art in itself and Harvey is usually able to place the field close to the action but out of the huntsman's way. When the hounds are running Harvey likes to be up with the action, 'I could never ride at the back,' he says with a laugh.

At Egmont-Wanganui children are encouraged to hunt. 'They are not allowed to hunt up the front,' Harvey explains. 'But they are allowed to hunt in the next wave, behind the senior riders. We have three pony club hunts and on those days the children can hunt up front if they wish. We encourage and look after them.'

Landowners are one of the most important components of hunting, as without them there would be no hunting. Harvey appreciates this. 'We are fortunate that we enjoy good relationships

* White electric tape is often used on dairy farms to restrain stock. It is highly visible and relatively straightforward to jump.

Egmont-Wanganui members on a run
in South Taranaki.

with our landowners. For example, as part of our centenary celebrations in 1994, I wanted to hunt over dairy country because dairying is such an important part of our region. I was dreading asking the dairy farmers if they would let us come because I knew there would be a large number of riders, but they all said "we would be honoured".

'We try to respect the landowners' property as much as possible and we make sure that any damage is repaired. About two years ago I got carried away when hounds were running and we went somewhere we weren't particularly welcome. I had to eat humble pie and ride over to the owner's house to apologise. I received a thorough ticking off – much to the field's mirth!'

Landowners are always invited to the hunt breakfast and looked after by members. A function for property owners is held annually in conjunction with the hunt's point-to-point meeting. 'We're probably gaining more properties than we lose,' says Harvey. 'Some hunts become concerned if there is an increase in dairy farming in their area. We don't because we have always been a dairying area and hunting can co-exist with dairy farming. We build railed spars when we can and we jump a lot of tape. Often the property owner will be hunting with us and when we get to something tricky he'll say, "Go for your life".'

Harvey is quick to emphasise that the fun of hunting is chasing the hare, not killing her. 'We don't make a big thing of the kill and I have never blooded anyone,' he says.

For Harvey and Ann, life with horses is a whirlwind of show jumping competitions during the summer culminating in the Horse of the Year Show in mid-March. Then they start hunting in the last weekend in March and continue through to early July. 'It is a busy life,' says Harvey, 'and some years it might take a few hunts to get the enthusiasm up, but it is fun!'

CHAPTER FOUR

A HUNTSMAN'S DAY

WITH HUNTSMAN LAURYN ROBERTSON OF WAIKATO HUNT

EACH HUNTSMAN HAS HIS OWN STYLE when he hunts. Some differences are influenced by the type of country, including the terrain and the proximity of boundaries, bush, plantations and roads. Other differences come from the individual preferences of the huntsman – for example, whether he will lift his hounds to move them if a hare is sighted. However, as hunting depends on the same ingredients of property, hounds and scent there are more common themes than differences. Waikato Huntsman Lauryn Robertson agreed to describe a hunting day from his perspective, although he stated that his style and preferences may not be the same as those of his peers.

Lauryn's entire working life has involved horses and dogs. His career started as a shepherd on New Zealand's rugged high country with a team of working dogs and farm hacks. While he was shepherding in the Mahia district, in the remote East Coast region of the North Island, good friend and local huntsman Harvey Wilson invited Lauryn to help him as whipper-in. Lauryn found that hunting combined his love of horses and dogs and he became passionate about the sport. He spent a lot of time learning about the profession from Hawke's Bay Huntsman Murray Thompson. Then, when Harvey moved to a new position in 1993, Lauryn took over as Mahia Huntsman.

The Mahia Hunt has a reputation for producing good huntsmen. It is a rural-based hunt where many members are steeped in hound knowledge, and during a day's hunting people observe the huntsman's every move. Mahia members are fiercely proud of their hounds and have high standards for a day's hunting. However, Mahia Hunt can only provide huntsmen with seasonal employment, so in 1999 Lauryn moved to a full-time position at the Waikato Hunt after long-serving incumbent Ron Cropp retired.

The Waikato Hunt is located in the central North Island, close to New Zealand's largest inland

Above: Waikato Huntsman, Lauryn
Robertson, at Arapuni.

Far left: Waikato hounds heading home
after an autumn hunt.

city of Hamilton. Waikato is one of New Zealand's most abundant pastoral farming regions with
an emphasis on dairy and meat production and equestrian activities, including a number of pros-
perous thoroughbred stud farms. The countryside is wonderfully green, undulating, with lots of
trees and dissected by lazy brown rivers winding their way to the coast. There are several hunts in
close proximity including King Country, Maramarua, Taupo and Rotorua Bay of Plenty.

Lauryn's performance, as with other huntsmen throughout the country, is primarily judged
on hunting days. This is when the huntsman's hard work throughout the year, breeding, training,
feeding and preparing hounds and horses, must come together.

Lauryn likes to select his hounds the evening before the hunt. 'I base my selection on the
individual hound's condition, whether it is sound, and the experiences it has had at recent hunts,'
he says. 'I also think about the type of country we are going to hunt and select the numbers and

type of hound accordingly. If it is a smaller property, with a lot of bush, I may take a smaller pack of older, more experienced hounds. Normally I take about fourteen couple.'*

Lauryn feeds his hounds carefully the day before the hunt. 'I believe the feeding of the hounds is important and I like to feed mine early the day before they are due to hunt. I give the young hounds and lightweight hounds free access to the food, but I restrict the grosser types.'

As well as the quality of the hounds, a huntsman is assessed on his horses and horsemanship. A huntsman is expected, within reason, to be able to follow the line of the hounds. For Lauryn, in the Waikato region, this can include negotiating a range of jumps from prepared spars and lowered wires to hedges, full wires with electric fence outriggers and high tensile fences with no battens. Fences without battens are particularly challenging as it can be difficult for horses to sight the fence, especially when the winter sun is low in the sky and the wire is high tensile which is relatively thin.

On a hunting day the huntsman is like a conductor bringing together the orchestra of hounds and horses to entertain and provide sport for the followers. His day is a long one. 'On the morning of the hunt I rise early and let the selected hounds out for a run in the hound paddock. I feed and prepare my horses. I also prepare the feed for the horses and the hounds on their return so they can be fed as soon as I arrive back. Normally it's dark by then so preparation is important.

'I like to arrive at the meet at least one hour before the hunt moves off so I've got time to talk with the property owner and the master. It is important to understand what country is available, particularly in relation to the property owner's grazing requirements. If necessary, I talk to the whippers-in about any hounds they should watch for. Maybe some hounds have been working wide, or chasing animals other than hares.' Sometimes in the Waikato on the smaller properties the whippers-in need to be aware of the property boundaries, including road hazards.

'When I let the hounds out of the truck I like them to be packed up while the master greets the field and announces the conditions for the day. I will then ride to the country I want to draw first. Sometimes the property owner or the master may choose this, otherwise huntsmen learn to know which country is more likely to have hares. In fine weather, I look for suitable cover, be it a hedge line or a wood plantation. If it has been raining and the weather has recently cleared, the hares will probably be out in the open.'

During the hunt, Lauryn's concentration is on the hounds. 'I watch the hounds all the time, especially the older experienced hounds who I know I can trust. I am watching their movements: Are their noses down? Are they working a line? Are they making noise?

Right: A King Country field watches as the hounds hunt out of bounds.

* Hounds are usually counted in couples. A couple is two hounds and 'half a couple' is one hound.

'If I see a hare jump up I believe it is the ultimate sin to pick the hounds up and take them to the spot. I like to let them draw there. If a huntsman picks his hounds up they never hunt the hare as well as if they are allowed to draw there. It's my belief that the less the hounds' heads are lifted, the better they scent.

'When the hounds are running my job is easier. But it is important to watch for any signs of a check. I watch my leading hounds. A good hound stops speaking when the scent stops. A younger, less experienced hound may overrun. When the hounds check I like to wait and see if they can find the line of scent without me intervening. If they can't then I help. The hardest days are when the scenting conditions are difficult. One hare on a good scenting day can provide good sport. But on a difficult scenting day all the hares in the world may not help. Sometimes the scenting conditions can be variable throughout the day. For example, on a windy day the scent may be all right in sheltered areas, or on hot days the scent may hold in shady places. Sometimes the scent may improve later in the day as the temperature drops. It is such a variable part of the sport.'

Lauryn has some dislikes when he is hunting. 'One is jumping fences with electric fence outriggers on both sides. Another is people sitting on top of a ridge hollering that the hare has gone a certain way. It can distract hounds and then they lift their heads. These people overlook the purpose, that we are there to let the hounds hunt the hare.'

For the Waikato Hunt the day ends when the master decides. 'It is usually based on when the hounds or the field have had enough. Early in the season when it is hot the hunts need to be shorter. We make up for it around the end of June. If the weather's good and the hunting is going well there is nothing wrong with staying out for an extra half hour.

'On the way in, either one of the whippers-in or I will count the hounds, and I will run my eyes over them, checking for lameness or injury. Then they are trucked up and I attend to my horses.

'Before the hunt breakfast I choose which hounds have earned points in the "Hound of the Day" competition. My decision is based on which hounds have worked well at checks, or worked hard on a tough line or in difficult scenting conditions.'

Above: Taranaki Master Kevin Zimmerman
leads the field on a run.

Lauryn enjoys the chance to relax at the hunt breakfast and chat with members about the day. However, after the breakfast there are chores to complete before his day is over. 'I like to get home as soon as possible and feed my animals and get them back to their paddocks and kennels. There is saddlery to clean, the hunt truck to tidy, and maybe injured animals to care for. At the end of the day I'm usually mentally exhausted, especially on a difficult scenting day.' Lauryn keeps a record of each hunt, including how the property hunted and details of good hound work, for future reference.

Hunting in the Waikato is carded two, sometimes three, times a week so the months from April to July are busy ones for Lauryn, his horses and his hounds.

82

Above: Hawke's Bay hounds benefit from a well-earned drink watched by Huntsman Murray Thompson.

Far left: Waikato's Emma working a line.

Left: A South Canterbury hound struggles through a tightly wired fence.

Far right: Moving out to draw: combined Waikato and Rotorua-Bay of Plenty packs.

A pack of hounds is a wonderfully happy community and we love to watch them,
to see them go in answer to their instincts, and try to keep near them on a horse we cherish,
over fence and ditch. That is HUNTING to us, nothing else.

Captain Douglas Bingley in *A Great Run*

Above: Taranaki members wait at a check on Jeremy Thomson's award-winning agroforestry property in East Taranaki.

Above left: Waikato hounds casting.

Below left: Manawatu members follow the action, watched by an absorbed audience.

The end of the day for Taranaki Hunt.

CHAPTER FIVE
A MASTER'S VIEW OF A HUNTING YEAR

WITH MASTER GLYNNE SMITH OF CENTRAL OTAGO HUNT

THE YOUNGEST HUNT IN NEW ZEALAND is Central Otago, founded in 1989, in the southern part of the South Island. The history of the Central Otago hunt makes for interesting reading. It was started by a group of enthusiasts, including Glynne Smith, who were tired of travelling huge distances to hunt with the nearest pack of hounds. As Glynne drove through his home district in the vast Central Otago tussock country, his son Jonathan commented that he was sure it would be possible to set up a hunt closer to home and save on travel expenses. Other people supported the idea and several hunts offered to contribute hounds.

Glynne was inspired by the challenge and the first meeting to gauge enthusiasm was convened on 5 July 1988. The impetus grew and portable kennels were constructed in February 1989 ready for the eagerly awaited arrival of the first hounds. The nucleus of a superb little pack was drafted to Central Otago with representatives of some of the oldest and best bloodlines in the county. Glynne, then aged 50, was elected as amateur-huntsman and master and had the challenging task of welding the varied pack into a working unit. He was no stranger to working with dogs as he had competed in dog trials, but that was a one-on-one partnership as opposed to the pack situation where the huntsman has to be top dog. The more Glynne worked with the hounds, the more passionate he became about the role.

Fortunately Glynne's family was supportive of the new hunt. Glynne's wife Lynley took up riding in her adult years so she could enjoy the sport that has enthralled her husband and their sons Jonathan, Charles and Phillip.

Above: Glynne Smith and Huntsman Lloyd Brenssell discuss the country and hunting prospects.

Right: The Central Otago field watch the hounds and huntsman ride out at the start of a mid-week meet at Clyde.

Above left: President Mac Wright takes to the saddle using a stool for a mounting block.

Above right: Vicky Roberts works on some running repairs.

Far right: Joanna Huddleston shelters from the rain.

The founding committee was a group of enthusiastic locals all keen to see hunting thrive in Central Otago – and so it has. The hunt boasts some of the best sporting country in New Zealand, with vast river terraces in big valleys, huge paddocks and brilliant scenery. Central Otago is sparsely populated, often dry and brown and overwhelmingly beautiful. The vista is dominated by mountain ranges that rise above the terraces with jagged edges and deep snowcaps in winter. Covered with native tussock and outcrops of massive schist rocks, the country has a wild, untamed appearance.

Glynne Smith has been dedicated to the Central Otago Hunt since those first days. Although he handed over the huntsman's coat after five years he has continued as master and is now one of the most experienced in New Zealand. Central Otago Hunt is one of the smallest in New Zealand with a membership of 47. Huntsman Lloyd Brenssell is employed on an amateur basis and the hunt is held together financially by the members' ingenious fundraising methods. Like many small hunts there is a strong sense of camaraderie and pride among the supporters. Lloyd comments, 'It is a happy hunt where everyone quietly works together without hierarchy to ensure that things get done.' Much of the credit belongs to Glynne who has the rare ability to have a relaxed leadership

style while still ensuring that important matters are addressed. He is affable, accommodating and has an ever-present sense of humour. One of Glynne's favourite sayings is 'Until you learn to laugh at yourself you don't get anywhere in this world'. Glynne and Lynley have a reputation for providing the warm hospitality for which South Islanders are famous.. They live in a nineteenth century converted stone cottage in Middlemarch and many of their social and sporting activities revolve around hunting.

The master's year starts with the annual general meeting in November where Glynne has been elected unopposed every year. 'After the AGM our first task is to convene a meeting to organise the dates for all the winter hunting and arrange the production of the hunt card,' he says. 'We try to include one new property on the card each year. If it hunts well we keep it on the card.'

Committee members take responsibility for organising the hunts in their locality, including liaison with the property owners and preparing country. This means Glynne's job is much simpler and entails overall coordination. 'Our opening meet is normally carded for the middle of March, although it is changing because the weather is so hot then (around 26 to 28 degrees centigrade) and the ground is hard and dry. But we need to finish our season early, around the end of June, because the weather becomes cold and the ground freezes.' To compensate for the short hunting season many weekend meets are carded with hunting on both Saturday and Sunday, which may include overnight stays at a local hotel or in the shearers' accommodation at a farm.

'During the year President Mac Wright and I stay in regular contact with Huntsman Lloyd Brenssell,' continues Glynne. 'We talk about how the hounds are working and any problems he is having, and Lloyd might ask me for my opinion on any breeding matters. I always go to the South Island Hound Show and I think it is important to support both the show and our huntsman's contribution. It is one of the few events where all the South Island hunts meet together, and the social intercourse is good for hunting.

'The relationship between the huntsman and the master is very important. It is hard to put it into words. We have to pull together.' Lloyd has been the Central Otago huntsman for three seasons and has nothing but praise for Glynne. 'I know if I have a problem or something needs sorting out Glynne will always do it.' he says. 'Nothing is a problem for him. He is so easy going, a really nice guy and a brilliant master.'

Landowners are essential to hunting and Glynne acknowledges this. 'We could not operate without them. Before we started hunting in Central Otago the landowners didn't understand what hunting was about. Many landowners couldn't comprehend that a group of people would want to

spend time galloping about chasing a hare when a greyhound and a shotgun would be more effective, but despite this they are open to the hunt using their properties. When we first set up not one property owner turned us down.

'We have tried to introduce a landowners' social event but they are often reluctant to accept our hospitality as they think the hunt is too poor to be able to afford it. So I buy the landowners a drink when I see them at a stock sale or the rugby or any other social occasions. Most landowners come to the hunt breakfast and have a bite to eat and a drink with us. The landowners and their children hunt without paying a cap (the fee hunts may charge visitors to participate in a day's sport).

'I like hunting the native country in Central Otago. The rocks, the gullies and the tussock country with vast 200-acre [81-hectare] paddocks appeals to me as opposed to small farms with lots of jumping. We do not hunt over any dairy country, and although many of our hunting properties have a lot of high country we only hunt the lower parts. I am passionate about the country here and I feel at peace when I'm out there among the tussock and rocks.

'All our country is well prepared,' continues Glynne. 'This helps encourage people to try hunting and it helps encourage parents to send their children hunting.' The inaugural hunt committee developed an ingenious way to make the netting and barbed wire fences more jumpable by using portable rails with hooks that loop over the top wire of a fence. Using this method vast areas can be sparred efficiently and quickly.

Glynne attends the annual general meeting of the New Zealand Hunts' Association in Wellington every July. 'Each master presents a brief report on their hunting year. Every hunt every year has had a fantastic season and every member is a fantastic member!' says Glynne with a smile. 'The greatest benefit of this meeting is chatting with the other masters and learning about how they have overcome any problems or managed their fundraising.'

Often good fundraising ideas will be used by other hunts, including stock schemes, summer treks and hound auctions. A stock scheme is where the hunt either purchases or is gifted weaner calves, which are then grazed for free by members and friends of the hunt. Profits from the cattle sales support the hunt's finances. Sometimes there is talk about swapping hounds. Other agenda items can include the relationship between hunting and racing, the hunting situation in the United Kingdom and the outcome of any disputed boundary discussions.

'Bessie [Fullerton-Smith, the NZHA patroness] is always there and always very interested in our hunt's progress. And then we depart, slapping each other on the back and swearing eternal friendship until next year!'

*I think very few members realise just how much work is entailed in being a master. ...
Take the relationship between the hunt and the property owners, without whose cooperation
there would simply be no hunting; this most vital work is almost entirely the master's and
never ceases... it is the master, in the final analysis, who is responsible for the country hunted
over, not only in its acquisition, but in its keeping by ensuring that the owners' wishes,
their crops and fences are respected...*

Duncan Holden in *Harking Back II, A History of Hunting in New Zealand 1870–1989*

As Central Otago is a small hunt, the members' subscriptions only cover a part of the hunt's expenses, so fundraising activities are critical to the hunt's survival. 'We pick fruit and cut firewood, we've organised gymkhanas, we still organise raffles, we do the car parking at the Queenstown rodeo, and we even put the stonework around the bottom of rabbit fences when rabbits were a major problem in the area,' says Glynne. Future plans include establishing a stock-grazing scheme.

Most of the hunt's social activities are focused around hunting. 'Because we have a short season we decided we would rather have lots of hunting days, then have social days at other times of the year,' Glynne explains. 'So when we organise weekend hunts we incorporate social activities including dinners and social get togethers.'

Glynne always ensures he has suitable horses in work to lead the field on a hunting day. His horses benefit from participating in a range of activities during the summer months including the local cavalcade in February, and jumping and dressage work at the local shows and one-day events, where Glynne has enjoyed much success. By the time the opening meet comes round his horses are fit and ready to gallop and jump. Hares are generally plentiful and the country demands a degree of boldness in both horse and rider. Inevitably the season flies by all too quickly.

Chapter Six

A Huntsman's Year

With Huntsman David Ferriman of Christchurch Hunt

THERE ARE TWO PARTS to a huntsman's job. There is the glamorous public side when the huntsman, resplendent in red coat, white breeches and gleaming black boots, is the focus of attention on a hunting day. And there is the less public side — the day-to-day routines of feeding and caring for hounds and horses and maintaining the kennels and other facilities. Animals require seven-day-a-week attention, regardless of the weather, public holidays or other considerations. There are hounds to breed, puppies to train, new horses to educate and maybe some public liaison roles to undertake. The success of these jobs underpins the quality of hunting during the winter season.

One man who excels in both aspects of the job is Christchurch Huntsman Dave Ferriman. Dave has been responsible for the Christchurch hounds for 29 seasons and has provided excellent sport for members throughout this period. He has presented seminars on kennel management to enthusiastic young huntsmen, and in this chapter he shares his experiences of a huntsman's year.

Hunting is a shared passion for the Ferriman family. Dave's wife Jan enjoys the sport, as do their three daughters Ann, Marie and Belinda. The entire family is involved in looking after the horses and hounds, and after a good hunt there is a shared feeling of pride.

The Christchurch Hunt was founded in 1880, although the first efforts to establish a hunt in the region date back to 1866. One of the earliest challenges was distributing hares throughout the farmland before hunting could take place. The local acclimatisation society assisted by selling hares caught by greyhounds in Christchurch City's Hagley Park for a pound apiece. Generous farmers offered the hunt vast properties to hunt over and the new sport thrived. Farming has since intensified around many parts of Christchurch, which has restricted access to some properties; but there is still a lot of available flat land that lends itself to fast-paced hunting, and there is an abundance of

Far right: Riding in at the end of the day — and the season. Dave Ferriman leads the hounds in at the Christchurch closing meet at Hororata.

Left: Dave Ferriman discussing progress with Brackensfield Huntsman Daf Davies.

Far right: Christchurch members at the check during Christchurch's closing meet. Top left: John Macer, top right: Master David McConchie, bottom left: Rob Elworthy, bottom right: (left to right) Jim Cassidy, Denis Hazlett, Jessica Elworthy and Len Insoll.

hares. Many paddocks are divided by gorse hedges and irrigation ditches that demand big bold jumping. There are also many tight netting fences with metal standards; hounds are encouraged to leap over these, otherwise progress is slowed.

Huntsman Dave Ferriman's year revolves around the hounds and their needs. He is also responsible for farming the hunt property of 65 hectares at Aylesbury, about 35 kilometres from Christchurch, and keeps horses in training throughout the year. When the Christchurch hunt season finishes in mid-July, most members turn their horses out and focus their attention on other activities. However, Dave and his family still have the hounds' care uppermost in their thoughts as they require daily attention and regular feeding. 'I collect old or unwanted horses and cattle for hound tucker on a weekly basis,' says Dave. 'The hunt owns a big freezer that can hold a stockpile of meat, and supply does not seem to be a problem.'

Many of the kennel routines are constant throughout the year. Dave's other jobs vary with the seasons, and include the management of the hunt property. In spring there is lambing to attend to, along with the ploughing and sowing of crops, which are harvested in autumn. Farm maintenance, including fencing and pasture management, is attended to during the months when there is no hunting.

Christchurch closing meet.

Huntsmen are judged on their horsemanship, and Dave spends a lot of time preparing young horses and competing during the summer months. Huntsmen are often sent problem horses, and many of those that were sent to Dave have developed into talented jumpers and hunters. He likes to free jump his horses in a specially constructed lunge arena to assess their ability and to give them the opportunity to develop a natural jumping style. The spring shows begin in October. Dave has had considerable success in hunter jumping and working hunter classes, and Ann, Marie and Belinda enjoy competing in a range of events. The Christchurch Agricultural and Pastoral Show in November is always a highlight. Competing is a family effort and there is a shared sense of camaraderie in the Ferriman team.

Dave, like many other New Zealand huntsmen, is the clerk of the course for local race meetings.

He attends 56 racing days a year for the Christchurch Jockey Club and Addington Raceway and always ensures he has at least one grey horse in work with the right temperament for the job, which includes accompanying winners to the weigh-in area or catching loose horses. Most of the racing is spread throughout the year, but during November there is an eight-day period with five days of racing. This period coincides with the Christchurch Show, so November is always a busy month.

Dave starts working on the hounds' fitness in mid-February, eight weeks before the opening meet in mid-April. 'I start by walking the hounds for six to eight kilometres along the road verges. We are lucky here as there are good wide verges and little traffic. It is usually hot and dry and the ground is hard, so it is important that the hounds get access to the water races alongside the roads as they work up. I also take the hounds across the farm to teach the new entrants to negotiate the fences, which can include netting and gorse. The hunters start work around the same time if they haven't already been attending shows or doing "clerk of the course" work.'

In the past Jan helped Dave exercise the hounds, but more recently a part-time assistant has been helping out. Otherwise Dave and his family manage all of the hound and horse work themselves.

Dave is responsible for making any breeding decisions for the pack. 'I like to breed my bitches to whelp during the hunting season, ideally in May,' he says. 'In this way the puppies will be ready to start working up the following autumn ready to hunt in the winter.' This is a different approach to most North Island hunts but has worked well for Dave. 'I like to breed about two litters each season and I leave a maximum of six to seven puppies on each bitch. Most of the time all the puppies go out to be walked by members when they are weaned at eight weeks. I encourage the walkers to send the puppies back when they start doing the things that the walker doesn't want them to do but I do, such as putting their noses on the ground, working a line and wandering off hunting.'

There is usually a hound show scheduled for late March and Dave has enjoyed considerable success over the years. The Christchurch bitch Capture, which Dave bred and trained, won the supreme title at the New Zealand Hound Show in 2000. Dave spends time in early March ensuring that the hounds selected for the show lead well and are in prime physical shape. He finds that the hounds that have been walked are well socialised and this helps a lot.

By late March the hounds are ready for puppy hunting. The opening meet is carded for mid-April. Occasionally the dry Canterbury summers have delayed the start of hunting, as the ground can be hard at this time of the year and farmers suffering from autumn droughts and pasture shortages may be reluctant to host the hunt. However, when the season starts it is guaranteed that the hounds and horses in the Ferriman team will be fit and ready to go.

Above: Hounds of the Dannevirke Kennels.

Far right: Hounds of the Waikato Kennels.

Below: Christchurch hounds enjoying a drink.

Each season has its joys, 'tis true
And none should wisdom spurn,
But those who nature rightly view
Enjoy them each in turn:
The angler, racer, courser, shot
As each to each is borne;
But the season of seasons, is it not
When the huntsman winds his horn?

From *Weekly News*, May 1874

Ready to move off: Christchurch Huntsman
Dave Ferriman at the closing meet at Hororata.

Christchurch Hunt is bordered to the north by Brackenfield Hunt.

Below: Just like their neighbours, Brackenfield members enjoy the challenge of jumping big gorse hedges.

Above: During a check in the action, riders
enjoy a quick drink from their hip flasks
at a hunt near Rangiora.

Left: Brackenfield hounds move off at the start
of an autumn hunt.

Christchurch Hunt's southern neighbour is the South Canterbury Hunt.

Above: 'Gone away'– South Canterbury hounds pursue a hare down a country road.

Left: South Canterbury members Bridget Williams and Polly McDonald enjoy a champagne breakfast, kiwi-style, at their closing meet at Rangitata.

Right: Huntsman Ryan Smith galloping during a run.

South Canterbury riders clear
a demanding full-wire fence
off a gravel road.

CHAPTER SEVEN

A Day in the Life of a Whipper-in

WITH WHIPPER-IN JOHN LOZELL OF THE PAKURANGA HUNT

A WHIPPER-IN ASSISTS THE HUNTSMAN to control the hounds on hunting days. A good whipper-in acts in an unobtrusive yet authoritative manner to influence the hounds to go where the huntsman wants. An old sage once said a good whipper-in is like a good eye-dog – watching, controlling, and influencing in a quiet yet effective way without loud noises or cracking whips.

In New Zealand whippers-in are amateur riders who assist the huntsman on hunting days only. They differ from their European counterparts, who may also help in the kennels. Typically there are two whippers-in on a hunting day, one on each side of the hounds with the huntsman in the middle.

Being a whipper-in can be a demanding job, yet there are usually several volunteers. One of New Zealand's most experienced whippers-in is John Lozell, who has assisted Pakuranga Huntsman Ross Coles for nineteen years.

John is a composite horseman with experience across practically every equestrian-related activity. As a child he competed in show jumping and horse trials, and hunted with the Egmont Wanganui Hunt, where he developed an early love of the sport. He represented New Zealand in polocrosse as captain of the national team on a tour of Australia and New Guinea in 1978. John also played polo for many seasons and in 1987 was a member of an Auckland team that won the Saville Cup, rated as New Zealand's premier polo competition. John worked for Cody Forsyth, who has been the country's leading polo professional, preparing polo ponies and playing to a four-goal handicap. Additionally, John rode saddle bronco horses and was a 'pick-up' rider on the North Island rodeo circuit for six years. Currently he is clerk of the course for several Auckland racing clubs and operates an equine sea freight business in partnership with his wife Alison.

John started hunting with the Pakuranga Hunt in 1981 when Ross Coles' father, Ray, was the

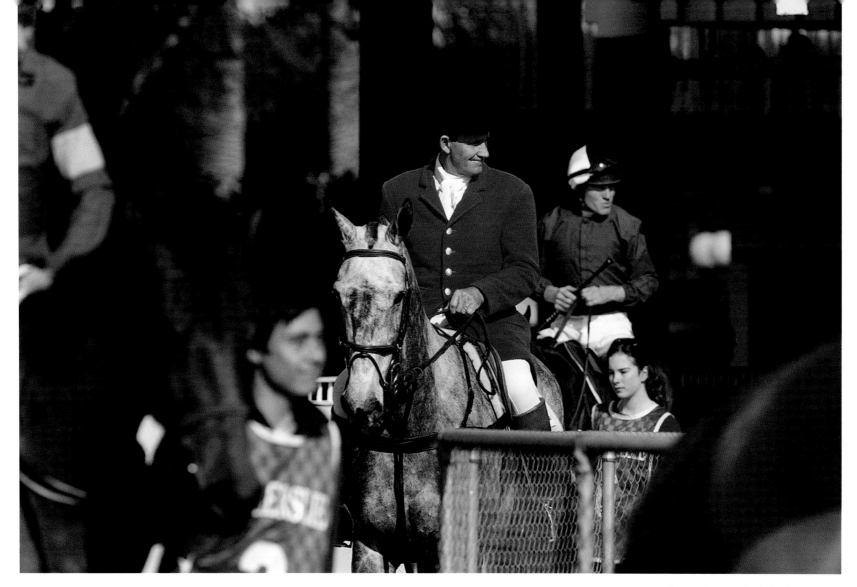

Above: John Lozell, Clerk of the Course, at an Auckland Racing Club meeting at Ellerslie.

huntsman. Ray quickly recognised John's horsemanship skills and invited him to help as whipper-in. 'I have always liked hunting,' says John, 'And as whipper-in I love the extra challenge of going where the hounds go. I like jumping testing fences and watching the hounds work. I especially enjoy observing the hounds' progress from when they first start hunting as new entrants. It is always exciting when a young hound develops into a good hunting hound.'

Both John and Pakuranga Huntsman Ross Coles have clear views on the role of the whipper-in and the relationship between the huntsman and whipper-in. 'There are several important qualities for

There is more to the true spirit of hunting than owning the right horse, wearing the right outfit and turning up at the right time. If you never have felt the raw excitement of a horse whose heart matches yours, never felt the sting of rain in your face, never known the sweetness of a run, never felt affection for the hare that gave you sport then got away, then I would argue that you have hunted, but without ever having grasped the essence of what hunting really is.

Laraine Sole in *Gone Away, One hundred years with the Egmont-Wanganui Hunt Club*

Below: Pakuranga whipper-in, John Lozell enjoys a quick refreshment.

whippers-in to have,' says John. 'Firstly, they've got to have a love of hunting and how the hounds hunt. Some people want to be a whipper-in because they want to ride out the front and jump, but that's not what the job is about. It is about being there to help the huntsman and to do what he wants, and it is about being interested in the hounds and their hunting.

'A whipper-in has to be able to ride well, because they have to be able to jump everything that comes along. A lot of people think that they can jump well enough, but it is a lot more difficult to jump out on your own, especially to jump going away from the field.

'Good whippers-in are quiet achievers. They do not need to yell and scream. Whippers-in hardly ever need to crack their whips. I only do if the hounds are out of bounds and I cannot get to them. Then I will crack my whip to lift their heads so I can get their attention and call them back to me.

'Good whippers-in are also good planners. For example, I am always thinking ahead about where the hare might have run, or where is the best place to jump out of a paddock.'

It is important to have an effective working relationship between the whippers-in and the huntsman. At the Pakuranga Hunt there are two principal whippers-in; the other is Russell Cartwright, who has been assisting Ross for about fifteen years. 'We know Ross well, he knows us, and the relationship works well,' says John. 'We can all make mistakes, but in Ross's case he will never abuse a whipper-in. He may come over and quietly explain how he wants something done, but he will never abuse anyone.'

Ross Coles adds, 'From my perspective it is important that I can trust my whippers-in and that we work together as a team. They need to have a large amount of hunting commonsense. If a person doesn't understand what the huntsman is trying to do then it is very hard. The whippers-in need to be ready to act, but look to the huntsman for their ultimate direction.

Waikato Whipper-in Paul Clarkin
negotiates a high hedge.

'Consistency is important to me,' continues Ross. 'My two [principal] whippers-in have been with me for a long time and we have a good relationship. They are both good whippers-in and their horsemanship plays a big part. Whippers-in need to ensure that they are horsed well enough to go anywhere. They have to be braver than brave. Both John and Russell are able to get to the hounds, if need be, and make them take notice of what they want.'

John has jumped some challenging fences during the years, including an imposing six-foot hedge while mounted on a young horse. Neither the horse nor John realised until they were airborne that there was a big wire fence on the landing side, just four metres from the hedge. Fortunately the horse had the courage to land and to immediately bounce over the wire fence. The field of around 120 riders watched in awe, in the belief that John had planned the whole thing!

From time to time, a person who rides in the field may have the opportunity to try their hand as a whipper-in. 'I would recommend that they go out with someone who is experienced,' advises John, 'and learn from them before they try to go out on their own. It is also important to talk to the huntsman and find out what commands he uses. Different huntsmen use slightly different commands.

'A whipper-in needs to know all the hounds' names. It is not something that you learn immediately. It takes time. Now that I know the whole pack, I only have to learn the new entrants' names at the start of each season. On a hunting day there are only a few hounds that need calling. Most of the hounds run in the pack and don't get into trouble, so they do not get called.

'One important job for the whippers-in is to count the hounds. I do it often throughout the day when the opportunities arise, for example when they are moving through a gateway. If a hound is missing it is the whippers-in responsibility to make sure it is found. I also watch the hounds to check that they are okay. Maybe one has a cut, or another looks sore, and I will mention it to Ross. Also, if I see a hound with its tail down I know that it is either sick or really tired, or it may have run out of bounds and received an electric shock from a fence.'

Far right: Ritchie Kennedy, amateur whipper-in for Waikato Hunt, assists Huntsman Lauryn Robertson at Te Akau.

Both Ross and John point out that different huntsmen use the whippers-in in different situations and in slightly different ways. 'Some of the differences are because they are hunting different country,' says Ross. 'For example, Murray Thompson, the huntsman for Hawke's Bay, has his whippers-in a lot further apart when he hunts. He hunts over bigger country with a larger pack and it is appropriate for him.' On a few occasions when Ross has been called away to manage New Zealand teams at major international competitions, John has hunted the hounds. He has thrived on the challenge, and no doubt Ross has been relieved to have a dedicated understudy to help out. Certainly, it is a pleasure to watch the team of Ross, John and Russell working together. They look professional and relaxed, and invariably set the tone for the people who follow.

Starborough hounds working a line on a tough, windy day at Grassmere.

Chapter Eight

Breeding a Pack of Hounds

With Huntsman Murray Thompson of Hawke's Bay Hunt

Murray Thompson has been huntsman for the Hawke's Bay Hunt for 33 seasons. In that time he has become a living legend among huntsmen in New Zealand. He is a colourful character, with a reputation for past exploits that make it difficult to decipher fact from fantasy. However, one constant throughout Murray's career has been his tremendous pride in his hounds. He has a bold breeding policy and the resulting pack of hounds has been rated among the best in New Zealand for their hunting ability, music and colour. They are an impressive pack to hunt behind.

Murray's life has been intertwined with hunting and hounds almost from the moment he was born. His father Hugh was a keen follower of hounds, and Murray started hunting when he was five years old. Hugh was Hawke's Bay huntsman from 1956–61, and it was no surprise when Murray applied for the same position in 1969. He was appointed on 13 October 1969, and so began his career of hunting the hounds in Hawke's Bay.

Hawke's Bay is a distinctive region on the east coast of the North Island. The mild climate, low rainfall and many hours of sunshine give the region a Mediterranean feel. This is extenuated by hundreds of hectares of vineyards that consume the flat lands, interspersed occasionally with fruit farms or horticulture.

Hawke's Bay Hunt was established in 1889 primarily by wealthy gentleman farmers who owned large land holdings in the area. There was great scope for hunting and much enthusiasm among early members. Initially most of the land hunted over was flat to gently rolling, but as viticulture has expanded the hunt has been pushed out to steeper, less intensively farmed land. Hunting in the Hawke's Bay midweek is not for the faint hearted as much of the country is unprepared and the fences are big and unrelenting. Murray leads the way with style, and observers are not surprised

Far right: Hawke's Bay hounds casting at Maraekakaho.

Once the puppies are born Murray may reduce the litter to a size the bitch can manage and he will treat them for parasites every ten days. The puppies are usually weaned at eight weeks of age.

Keen hunt members walk the puppies before they are returned to the kennels for their early education. Murray has designed an obstacle course to help train the young entry to cope with obstacles like fences, waterways and gates. The hounds have to negotiate a metre deep trough, steps and a six-wire gate in order to get to their food. Water is gradually added to the trough until finally the youngsters have to swim for their supper.

Murray starts working up the young hounds in early February when they are just over twelve months old as he prepares the pack for hunting for the new season. By the time the opening meet comes around in early April, the new entrants are fifteen to eighteen months old and ready to hunt.

'I like to breed fifteen or more pups each year,' he says. 'In two years time if five are left I'm doing well. I make decisions to cull on the basis of their temperament, and when they work up they must load in the truck. Some hounds don't like hunting with the field behind them and some are too wayward. Then I base the decision on their hunting ability, but if I like a hound I'm prepared to give it a chance over a couple of seasons.'

Over the years, as the Hawke's Bay Hunt have moved towards hunting in steeper country Murray has adjusted his breeding programme to ensure his hounds are suitable for that country. 'The hounds are not as heavy as they used to be,' he comments. 'Now they are leggier and a little taller and not quite as wide. The Hawke's Bay hounds got very fast for a while and that had to be toned down. I believe you need a good steady paced hound on the hill country, otherwise it is possible to lose the hounds.'

Murray attends the annual autumn hound show each year, and has enjoyed considerable success. He believes the hound shows are the backbone of hunting in New Zealand. 'Sometimes I joke about them, but seriously I think they are a great thing. Over time, the conformation of hounds in New Zealand has improved a lot. For example, in the old days many hounds were heavier and had flat feet. They struggled to stay sound. Nowadays it is not a problem; we have lighter hounds with much better feet that stay sound throughout their lives. Hound shows have helped a lot to improve the conformation.'

Murray would like to see new bloodlines imported to New Zealand to add to the existing houndlines here. 'There are pros and cons to importing a stud hound,' he says, 'but I'm all for it!'

Murray's typical enthusiasm is especially evident on hunting days. Former Dannevirke Huntsman Doug Isaacson comments, 'Murray is prepared to front with his horses and really hunt his hounds.

Through the centuries, by careful breeding and ruthless culling, the hound as we know it today, has been evolved.
The good hound must not only look the part, it must also be capable of doing it's terrific job: it must have a great
constitution to work and cover at speed very big distances every hunting day; good conformation to stand that work;
a wonderful nose to follow one scent among the enormous variety of scents encountered; the pack instinct,
an important attribute; and obedience and docility, yet the fire to hunt and to kill.
It is, as it should be, a wonderful creature.

Duncan Holden in *Harking Back II, A History of Hunting in New Zealand 1870–1989*

And on the day of the hunt, he will hunt and hunt. Dannervirke Hunt Master Barry Beatson visited the Hawke's Bay Hunt one day and was heard to comment "I know you fellows stay out late but I didn't know I had to bring my sleeping bag too!'"

Former Hawke's Bay Master Malcolm Coop says, 'The hardest thing is to get Murray to stop at the end of the day. If there is a hare to be hunted, he wants to keep hunting.' Malcolm Coop's successor Sam Nelson adds, 'Murray has a lot of ability to read a hare. He possibly even thinks like a hare and he knows their traits. On a difficult scenting day, in particular, this ability can enhance the day's hunting.'

Even after 32 seasons Murray's enthusiasm is as intense as ever. He is fortunate that his wife Pauline and daughter Deserae both support him in his role as huntsman. Pauline is an excellent rider and hunts regularly; Deserae works with Murray, helping him both with the horses and the hounds, and also hunts with her parents. This is a family committed to hunting and breeding top hounds in New Zealand.

Following pages: Hawke's Bay hounds with Murray Thompson, hunting into the dusk at Maraekakaho.

CHAPTER NINE

PUPPY WALKING

WITH PAST-MASTER SARA FISHER OF SOUTH CANTERBURY HUNT

Sara Fisher presents South Canterbury's champion stallion hound Isaac.

WHEN HOUND PUPS ARE WEANED they are often sent to hunt members' homes to be cared for and socialised. It seems like a fun job. A cute hound puppy arrives to be loved, played with and admired until it is ready to be returned to the huntsman. I thought it could be a good way of helping our local hunt, so I volunteered to walk an adorable tricoloured puppy called Damsel. Unfortunately the irresistible bundle turned into a shoe-chewing, bone-burying, garden-molesting, couch-sleeping terrorist. My two young sons Harry and Michael loved Damsel dearly and spent hours playing with her. Husband Mark did not have quite the same affection for her. His names for Damsel are not printable, and he celebrated when she was returned to the hunt kennels some months later. I, on the other hand, was prepared to sacrifice the odd shoe and flower bed for the pleasure of watching Damsel hunting. When she was old enough to hunt with the pack I could easily recognise her and delighted in watching her good work, shuddered when she misbehaved and silently cheered her on. I decided puppy walking is a rewarding role and have since cared for eight puppies of which several have developed into useful hunting hounds.

Every year dozens of hunt members throughout the country help out by caring for and socialising harrier hound puppies. One of the experts is South Island hunting enthusiast Sara Fisher. Sara was master of the South Canterbury Hunt from 1992 to 2000 and has a strong interest in breeding, hunting and showing hounds. Sara and husband Richard own and manage Shenley Station, a 3,850-hectare hill country farm in the McKenzie Country.

Taranaki's Axel in the kennels at Bell Block.

Hunting restores my vitality.
No matter how arduous the day's work or how long the committee meetings at night,
one day in the saddle restores my vigour. It is even evident in my step.

Sir Patrick Eisdell Moore.

The South Canterbury Hunt is one of New Zealand's smallest, with a membership of 45 people and a hunt carded on a weekly basis. It is located on the east coast of the South Island and covers a range of country from the Southern Canterbury plains through to rolling tussock-covered McKenzie Country. The hunt has struggled financially at times during its 120-year history, and the pack of hounds has varied in quality. However, over the last fifteen years the South Canterbury hounds have excelled in the field and the show ring, and Sara has been pivotal to this success. Along with amateur huntsman Ryan Smith she has set out to breed a pack of well-matched, sound hunting hounds. Sara is proud of the pack's success, which includes championship wins at South Island and New Zealand hound shows.

'Puppy walking is one of the most important stages of a hound's life,' says Sara. 'If it is not done well the puppies are never any good.' Caring hunt members walk all of South Canterbury's puppies. 'Walking hound puppies is basic good sense,' said Sara in her matter-of-fact way. She has had a lifetime of experience with working farm dogs, and husband Richard keeps terriers and pointers.

'Before a puppy goes out to be walked, Ryan Smith, our huntsman, talks to the people about what is required and the commands that the pup should be taught. The pups need to be taught to tie up, to lead and not to chase sheep or cats or chickens.' Sara laughs at her own comment, as there are no chickens left at Shenley Station, thanks to the efforts of the hound puppies and Richard's terrier.

'The puppies must be good with children,' Sara continues. 'We encourage children to lead and play with them. We want the pups to be treated as normal pet dogs during the time they are walked.'

Sometimes the puppies are sent out individually and sometimes as a couple. 'It depends on the person who is walking them. They are much easier to integrate back into the pack if they have gone out as a couple, but very few people can handle two hound puppies!' One huntsman summed it up when he said: 'Two puppies are always either going to or coming from trouble!'

One important part of puppy walking is knowing when to bring the puppies back to the pack. Hounds are hunting animals and they will chase anything that runs if they are not disciplined. 'As soon as the puppy walkers have any concerns, Ryan asks for the puppies to be returned,' says Sara.

Ryan also talks to the walkers about the hunt's culling policy. 'It is important for people to realise that their little darling may have to be culled if it doesn't perform,' says Sara. 'But it is done humanely and only for very good reasons.' Hunts have careful breeding programmes, so most puppies do succeed. Puppy walkers then have the pleasure of watching 'their' hounds hunting in the pack and maybe enjoying success at hound shows.

Showing hounds is a passion for Sara and something she takes pride in doing well. She spends a lot of time with the puppies that have been selected to show, teaching them to stand and lead well. 'Part of showing a hound well,' she explains, 'is ensuring that the hound is happy about standing up and having judges run their hands over its body. This is not natural for a hound. Teaching them to stand can be difficult, as they can be wriggly. I start by standing them up for short periods and then rewarding them generously. I gradually lengthen the time they stand. I am happy to use biscuits and bribery, and I like to make a fuss of the hound so it feels important.

'A big part of showing hounds is ensuring the puppies are walked by the right people. The hound should be taught to tie up and lead well including leading away from other hounds. It is time consuming to train a hound to stand well and very few huntsmen have that sort of time, especially when they have to find employment outside the kennels. We are fortunate in South Canterbury as our huntsman's mother, Anne Ryan, loves the hounds and helps with the puppies' preparation.'

Sara also places emphasis on the hounds' diet. 'I like to build their coats by feeding them eggs

133

Above: Dannevirke Hunt puppies.

Far left: A Dannevirke hound in full flight.

Above left: Margaret O'Leary is assisted by husband Michael, prior to presenting hounds at the Central Districts Hound Show. Michael is Huntsman for Wairarapa Hunt.

Above right: Competitors wait for the hound show to begin.

and oil to help bring out the shine. If they are well fed their coats look good. I also shampoo them the day before and use a super-white shampoo. On show day I spray their coats with a special spray to bring out the lustre and then I put a little baby oil around their eyes.

'The standard at the hound shows has improved considerably from the first shows that I attended. The huntsmen have a better attitude, and the trainability and the handling of the hounds has improved. I think it is good to get the hounds out in the public eye, and the conformation and presentation of hounds in New Zealand has improved as a consequence.'

Sara's enthusiasm and knowledge has no doubt contributed to the improvement. She has presented seminars to huntsmen on showing and is committed to presenting hounds to the highest standard.

Rangitikei Huntsman Bernard Illston leads a hound in the ring at the Central Districts Hound Show. Rangitikei enjoyed an excellent show, winning Supreme Champion with their entered bitch Secret, along with the Fullerton-Smith trophy for gaining the most points.

Chapter Ten

Judging at Hound Shows

With Philip Langdale, secretary and keeper of the New Zealand Harrier Hound Studbook

Hound shows were first introduced to New Zealand in the 1950s to help encourage correct conformation in hounds. The shows also provide a forum for huntsmen to meet and mingle; and if the noise level in the lunch tent is any indication, this is a success! Annual shows are held in both the North and South Islands and the National Hound Show is convened approximately every four years.

Philip Langdale, from Hawke's Bay, is one of New Zealand's foremost judges of hounds and also the secretary and keeper of the New Zealand Harrier Hound Studbook. The Studbook is published annually and contains a four-generation pedigree of every hound hunting in the country.

Philip is a staunch traditionalist with a dry wit and a vast knowledge of hunting and hounds. He and his wife Jane moved to New Zealand in 1976 from the United Kingdom. Previously Philip was field secretary for the Duke of Beaufort's hounds for four seasons, having been brought up hunting with the Cowdray in Sussex. He studied at Eton College where he learnt more about hare hunting as a whipper-in for the college's beagle pack than anything in the classroom. Jane was also a keen follower of hounds, and the pair met when hunting with the famous Scarteen hounds (the Black and Tans) in Ireland. Philip's introduction to hound judging occurred when he was asked to judge at the Dartmoor puppy show as a wedding present from their master and amateur huntsman Willy Poole. In turn, Willy came to New Zealand to judge the 1990 National Hound Show at Hawke's Bay and will be remembered by many New Zealanders as a witty raconteur.

Philip has definite thoughts on hound shows. 'It's important to remember that conformation is not the main ingredient in the selection of a sire or dam. Work is the first consideration and counts above looks. However, a well-made hound is likely to remain sound, move effortlessly and last

Philip Langdale.

longer. This is where the hound shows become useful, because judges must look for the qualities that sustain this.

'To enable a hound to move effortlessly it must be well balanced both when it is stationary and when it is moving. A good hound needs to be well muscled with good bone, so it gives the impression of having both strength and quality. Dog hounds should show masculinity and bitches should be feminine, and both should show presence.'

Philip has judged at many New Zealand hound shows and has an eagle eye when it comes to assessing conformation. When the hounds first enter the competition ring he looks at the overall

Rangitikei Master Jim Brice accepts the second
place rosette for the unentered doghound Vintage,
from Taranaki Past-Master Merv Laurence.
Hunt President Malcolm Grayling and the class
winner, Dannevirke Huntsman Andrew Wright,
look on.

Rotorua-Bay of Plenty Master
and hound show judge Bruce Calder
inspects a Taranaki hound presented
by Huntsman Keith Laurence.

There are no marks or points for hunting.
Nobody wins and nobody really loses but there is a certain sense of individual achievement
and this is probably not the same in any two people, or at different ages in the same person.
You don't ride at forty the way you did at twenty. And you ride differently again at eighty.
But while your weight and your joints and your eyesight will let you, you will still hunt.

Sir Patrick Eisdell Moore in *A Great Run*

picture and the hound's movement. 'A hound's front end must balance its back half so that it's weight is evenly distributed on all four legs. It should move freely with a long stride which will make it faster and give it better turning ability than a short striding hound. A good moving hound will have a laid back shoulder, which allows the foreleg to move forward with big straight strides. Crooked action produces a shorter striding hound that will suffer from uneven wear on its pads.'

He then considers each part of the hound's conformation. One of the most important aspects is a hound's feet, and many huntsmen swear by the adage 'no foot, no hound.' It is especially true where hounds run across a lot of dairy tracks or rocky country. The toes should be close together with round cat-like feet that run on to straight forelegs with good bone.

'I like to see a deep chest rather than a barrel shape for this contains the power house of the heart and lungs,' continues Philip. 'A judge should be able to place his or her flat hand (ten centimetres width) on the hound's chest with each foreleg touching it. I look for a hound with a muscular level back, strong loins and powerful hind legs. A 'chopped-off' back is a weakness. The hind legs should have well let down hocks to be able to pass the forelegs when galloping. Cow or sickle hocks do not allow this. The hound's stern [tail] should be well set on, long and rise over the back without the tip turning over too much. The latter fault is really only cosmetic, and a hound with such a fault is referred to as 'being a bit gay' in judging terms.

'The hound's head should be of a medium size with a bold forehead. It should have a straight and powerful muzzle with an even and regular scissor bite. In other words, the upper teeth should closely overlap the lower teeth. An under- or over-shot mouth is a fundamental fault; it is highly hereditary and the hound should never be used for breeding purposes. I like to see high-set ears that are broad and lie close to the cheek.

'Personally I don't have a preference for colour. There has been some controversy in New Zealand about the ideal height for a harrier hound, which was promoted as 21 inches [53.5 centimetres]. Different huntsmen prefer different heights depending on the type of country they hunt. I avoid entering that debate,' says Philip with a chuckle – he was instrumental in getting the controversial 21-inch rule removed from the New Zealand judging criteria.

The first hound shows in New Zealand were hosted by the Waikato Hunt and held in conjunction with the Waikato Agricultural and Pastoral Show in Hamilton in the immediate post-World War II period. Ray Coles can remember attending the shows, first in the capacity as a professional whipper-in and then as Pakuranga huntsman. He enjoyed considerable success over the years. Over time Ray has noticed a difference in the quality of hounds hunting and the consistency between packs. 'The conformation and soundness of hounds has improved enormously and a lot of the improvement can be attributed to the hound shows. Huntsmen today are a lot more aware of how correct conformation will influence the soundness and longevity of their hounds. Hound shows and the intelligent use of the Studbook are a very positive part of this.'

A Rangitikei hound waits for her class.

BESSIE FULLERTON-SMITH

PATRONESS OF THE NEW ZEALAND HUNTS' ASSOCIATION

IMAGINE A TALL AND EXTREMELY ELEGANT LADY who is articulate, vibrant, intelligent, and witty. Add to the recipe a lifetime love of hunting and sport, including golf and tennis. Throw in a good measure of charisma, that indefinable quality that some people possess. Last but not least, take into consideration that the lady in question is 95 years old and still physically fit, and you have Bessie Fullerton-Smith, the patroness of the New Zealand Hunts' Association.

Bessie is an icon of New Zealand hunting. She is universally admired and loved by the people who know her. Bessie's life has been intertwined with hunting. She started riding almost as soon as she could walk, and her father encouraged her to hunt with the Rangitikei hounds from a young age. Bessie loved the horses, hounds and the jumping, but she was kept busy with a range of sports including golf. She won two New Zealand Ladies Championships and travelled to Australia and Europe to represent New Zealand in international golf tournaments.

However, between the travel and golf training, Bessie continued to ride and hunt. During World War II she helped exercise the Rangitikei hounds, which were in the care of long-serving Huntsman Arthur Goodwin. Bessie learnt all the hounds' names and benefited from Arthur's vast knowledge of the sport. When hunting resumed after the war, Bessie was asked to be whipper-in, which was a role she loved. 'It is the best job,' said Bessie. 'Just wonderful. You can ride with the hounds and you never get into trouble.' Even when golf tournaments resumed and fixtures coincided, she seldom missed a hunt.

In 1954 Bessie became the first female deputy master in Rangitikei's history. Two years later she was elected master, a position she held for seventeen years. Author Jeanette Galpin, who penned a lively biography about Bessie's achievements, wrote 'Every rider who followed hounds with Rangitikei during the seventeen years of Bessie's mastership grew to love and admire this cheer-

Bessie Fullerton-Smith presenting the Olympic Rose Bowl to the winner of the Premier Class at the New Zealand Horse of the Year Show.

ful, upright woman who led so well and would take on any challenge. She was always on time, always perfectly turned out – and she expected punctuality, good turn-out [and] thoughtful behaviour from every member of the field.'

In 1962, Bessie instigated the first all-hound show hosted by Central Districts. Previously hound classes had been held in conjunction with the Waikato Agricultural and Pastoral Show in Hamilton, but the Rangitikei hound show set a new precedent.

Bessie was actively involved in a range of equestrian activities including jumping, showing and judging. She enjoyed a lot of success on a range of horses, the best of whom was the chestnut thoroughbred Royal Crest, gifted to Bessie by Sir Thomas Duncan. Riding Royal Crest she won the first One Day Event held in New Zealand back in 1954, when the Rangitikei Hunt organised the competition. Bessie also supported show jumping when it was introduced to New Zealand in the

1950s. She donated the Olympic Rose Bowl for the winner of the Horse of the Year competition in 1954 and she still attends the show each year to present the trophy.

On 8 November 1972, Bessie was awarded an MBE for services to equestrian sport. 'That decoration meant much more to us than I can say,' says Bessie, who attended the investiture at Government House with her late husband Rod, son Henry and his wife Chris. 'It was one of our proudest days.'

In 1973 Bessie retired as master, but her love of the sport remains. Fittingly, in the same year she was elected patroness for the New Zealand Hunts' Association. It is a role that she clearly enjoys, and she still attends the AGM of the NZHA in Wellington every July. Bessie continued hunting until 1994 and remained tall, proud and elegant in the saddle. She may have continued hunting for longer but leg problems forced the retirement of her pony Monty, so Bessie decided to retire too. She still follows the fortunes of the Rangitikei Hunt and other hunts throughout New Zealand and astounds people with her youthful enthusiasm. She sums it up completely with her attitude: 'I just love people,' she says. 'I love life!'

In 1992, at the age of 85, Bessie attended the Starborough Hunt closing meet. Jeanette Galpin recounts: 'After hunting all day Bessie attended the hunt's annual ball that night, and was still dancing the night away in the small hours.'

'I don't feel old,' Bessie said. 'I love being with young people. That keeps me young.'

David Withers

President of the New Zealand Hunts' Association

There is something special about meeting people who are passionate about their life and their sporting activities. As they talk, their enthusiasm permeates everything they say and their joie de vivre can be contagious. David Withers is a man who is enthusiastic about life, especially when it involves hounds, horses, people and the New Zealand countryside. David is the current president of the New Zealand Hunts' Association, and hunting with hounds is one of the loves of his life.

The object of the New Zealand Hunts' Association is to oversee the sport of hunting from a management and financial perspective. Every hunt in New Zealand can send a voting member to the annual general meeting held in July in Wellington, and the eight member management committee is elected at this meeting. The committee meets by teleconference four times a year and critical business over past years includes press liaison and monitoring the hunt situation in the United Kingdom.

David is a member of the Mahia Hunt on the East Coast of the North Island. He farms with his wife Gaye at Tuahu Station in the Ruakituri Valley under the shadow of the Urewera mountain range, where they have lived for 40 years. He has been President of Mahia Hunt since 1989, whipper-in for many a year, and one of five ward masters from 1995 to 2000.

David's view on hunting is clear. 'Hunting is all about hounds. Without hounds there is no hunting! People who hunt need to understand hounds and their natural instinct to scent. Members need to be passionate about their hounds. I am sure this must be helpful for huntsmen.'

For David, hunting epitomises his values of team spirit. 'I'm a great believer in team spirit and I like to promote it in everything I do, including rugby, Search and Rescue and the mustering gangs

New Zealand Hunts' Association President David Withers (right) discussing prospects at the Central Districts Hound Show with Manawatu President Barry Mansell.

I've worked with. Hunting involves a lot of team spirit too. There is the team of people following the hounds, and there is the pack of hounds.' All three of David and Gaye's children, Amanda, Bridget and Leigh, have hunted with Mahia Hunt, and their grandchildren, twins Brad and Damien MacPherson, were whippers-in for a time.

David's love of hunting stems from a lifetime interest in horses, dogs and the wilderness. 'When I was a boy I wanted to grow up and join the Royal Canadian Mounted Police. I read an article about how the police trained their own horses, worked with Alsatians and rode in the remote mountains. They were the things I wanted in my life – horses, dogs, mountains and being part of a team. I have always lusted for mountains and nature.'

Early in his working career David was introduced to the New Zealand Search and Rescue organisation and this has become another major theme in his busy life. 'In 1962, six interested people, including myself, developed a Search and Rescue Team for the Urewera mountains. Now it is a group of over 100 people and one of the strongest SAR groups in New Zealand.'

Search and Rescue work is another activity that combines some of David's greatest passions of people, mountains and teamwork. But it is hunting that adds the extra ingredients of hounds and horses. 'I started hunting when I met Gaye. Gaye's family farm is Tuahu Station where we farm now and the station has been hunted for five generations by the Mahia hounds.'

One Mahia member says, 'Tuahu is a long way away, so you don't go there to hunt for the day – you go for the weekend, and if you're lucky you've recovered by Tuesday!'

Gaye and David share a common love of horses, hounds and the rural lifestyle. They married in 1962 and still enjoy hunting together. Gaye currently competes in dressage where she has enjoyed considerable success including representing New Zealand. She used to participate in show jumping, winning the Lady Rider of the Year title in 1975.

Mahia Ward Master Bruce Goldstone describes David as an enthusiastic master and president. 'David puts his whole being into what he does, be it Search and Rescue, hunting, polo or whatever. He believes in young people being occupied and he gets huge enjoyment from young people enjoying hunting. David and Gaye's horse-truck has room for six horses, and David ensures that whenever he travels to a hunt the truck is full of local people off to enjoy a day out.'

When I asked David to tell me about some of his best days hunting he replied, 'Any day following hounds is a good one!' David has hunted with every pack in New Zealand – except Taranaki, and he has plans to attend their centennial celebrations in 2004. 'Hunting is a wonderful sport and it is a real privilege to get on a horse and follow a pack of hounds in New Zealand.'

LYELL McLAUCHLAN

MASTER OF STARBOROUGH HUNT

LYELL McLAUCHLAN IS A LIVING LEGEND among hunting folk in New Zealand. Before I met Lyell it was difficult to separate myth from reality. Could he really drink whisky like I had been told, party all night, care for the Starborough hounds, look like a 60 year old and be master of Starborough Hunt, all at age 88? This is an age when most people are retired or deceased, yet Lyell's energy and enthusiasm for life are incredible. He owns and manages an 81-hectare drystock farm, rides horses, and pursues his love of hunting with an untiring zest.

Starborough Hunt was established in 1947 and Lyell was the founding master and huntsman. Starborough is located in the Marlborough province at the top of the South Island. The region is notoriously dry, with brown hills dissected by stony riverbeds. There are fertile flatlands around Blenheim, which are covered with vineyards. Marlborough produces some of the best wines in the world, but the downside is that the local hunt is continually losing some of its best hunting country to viticulture. Despite this, the 90 members are enthusiastic, friendly and proud of their hunt. There is a strong acknowledgement that Lyell, who is master to this day, personifies the Starborough Hunt. It is appropriate, therefore, that the hunt's colours are the McLauchlan tartan.

Starborough is the only amateur family hunt in New Zealand. Everyone contributes time and expertise voluntarily, with the exception that Huntsman Peter Vavasour is paid a petrol allowance to cover his travel expenses to exercise the hounds. The hounds are still kennelled at Lyell's farm 'Balvonie' and cared for by Lyell, as they have been for 55 years. He makes all the breeding decisions, transports them to and from the hunts, and works them up with the huntsman prior to the

Starborough Master Lyell McLauchlan.

start of the season. Lyell was helped by his late wife Ailsa for many years and his three sons Keith, Bruce and John have assisted as whippers-in at various times.

In his heyday Lyell was a brave and straight-riding master. As age started to catch up with him he would lunge his horse over the fences and because of his excellent knowledge of the country he was still able to keep up with the action. However, during the late winter of 1997 he had a serious accident, the result of 'losing an argument with a crusty old breeding cow'. He suffered a ruptured spleen, punctured lung and broken ribs. For a while Lyell's life hung in the balance, but his recuperative powers amazed the doctors and he was back hunting with his beloved hounds the very next season, although he no longer jumps. Perhaps his recovery was due in part to the restorative qualities of whisky, which is Lyell's favourite drink and an integral part of the hunting breakfasts. However, one strict rule all Starborough members adhere to is that there is no alcohol consumed while hounds are hunting.

Nowadays on a hunting day, Lyell, resplendent in his red coat, leads the field to the first paddock where hounds draw. Then the two Deputy Masters, Bob Todhunter and Paul Rutherford, seamlessly take over the leadership. Lyell, often accompanied by long-time friend Mary Cameron, follows more sedately. As he rides he is always watching and listening to the work of his hounds. For Lyell, the music and hunting ability of his hounds is paramount. He loves his pack of eleven couple, but has no sentiment when it comes to making breeding and culling decisions. 'A hound must have an excellent hunting instinct and be full of music, otherwise it is no good,' he says. He is an advocate of line breeding and has repetitively bred back to his foundation lines.

On the Saturday in May that I hunted with Starborough over new country near Nelson, Lyell's hounds were frustrated by the lack of hares. He was determined that I should have the opportunity to hear the Starborough hounds' beautiful music and he was immediately planning more hunting. Should the hounds go out the next day, or an additional hunt be added to the card for the following Tuesday? Starborough members were supportive, and so the following Tuesday we met at Marshlands, near Blenheim. This time the conditions were much better and we were treated to

an excellent day's hunting with ample opportunity to listen to the joyful sound of the hounds' music. Lyell was buoyant with enthusiasm and justifiably proud of his hounds' ability.

The addition of an extra hunting day is typical of Lyell, whose appetite for hunting will seemingly never tire. One classic story recounts a day's hunting at Lyell's farm 'Balvonie'. The hounds hunted a hare long and hard, but at dusk she disappeared into a crop of chou moellier. The frustrated hounds were returned to the kennels and the riders suppered at the house and brooded over the hare's tactics. The frustration of the riders grew until Lyell, Pat Dillon, Tom Hood and Ken Radd returned to their saddles at midnight and released the hounds from the kennels. The hare was lifted almost immediately from the paddock by the chou and put up a merry chase. The riders galloped and jumped in the moonlight, racing from paddock to paddock, as the music from the hounds echoed through the night. Finally the hare loped across the main highway and the hounds were called off, as the riders agreed their match had been met.

This is one story of many that is typical of Lyell's life, which has been filled with adventures involving hunting and hounds. It is still difficult to distinguish fact from fantasy but, where Lyell is involved, expect the unexpected.

Above: Starborough hounds with Huntsman Peter Vavasour on a run, followed by Deputy Master Bob Todhunter, and the field at Grassmere.

Far left: Vicki Todhunter cleanly clearing a spar at a Starborough hunt.

Sir Patrick Eisdell Moore

Past-Master of Pakuranga Hunt

Occasionally one has the good fortune to meet someone who is truly inspirational. One such person is Sir Patrick Eisdell Moore, past master of the Pakuranga Hunt and retired ear, nose and throat surgeon who was knighted for his significant contribution to hearing in New Zealand. Although Sir Patrick is now in his eighties he is articulate and lively and it was a pleasure to sit and listen to him reminisce about hunting.

Sir Patrick Eisdell Moore's hunting experience is vast. He started as an eight-year-old, over 75 years ago, when his father took him hunting bareback on a little chestnut pony called Bubbles, who had a mouth like iron and was too small to jump the big hedges and ditches that the hunt encountered. From his humble introduction to the sport, Pat went on to be master of the Pakuranga Hunt from 1975 to 1985 and president of the New Zealand Hunts' Association from 1984 to 1988. He is now an emeritus member of the association and a life member of the Pakuranga Hunt.

Although declining health now prevents him from hunting, Sir Patrick still speaks passionately of his love for the sport. His aim as master was simply to encourage people to enjoy hunting. 'People coming out to hunt are primarily there to enjoy themselves, and it's the master's job to make sure they do,' he says. 'The huntsman's job is to find the sport and produce the run, and it is the master's job to ensure that everybody gets the best out of it. He does this by selecting the time that he takes off and the line that he rides while following hounds as closely as possible. It meant I was always watching the hounds, the huntsman and the fences and keeping in mind which fence I would lead the field over. Some of them would want to face formidable obstacles and some of them would not be up to it. I had to reduce as much as possible the potential for damage. When you get the hounds taking off quickly and the entire field is chattering you have a short time to decide where to go. It is difficult to put it down in writing how a master can encourage enjoyment while still maintaining a sense of etiquette, but it is possible.'

Sir Patrick was a member of the committee that organised the Pakuranga Hunt Centenary celebrations in 1972. As part of the celebrations he co-authored with Captain Douglas Bingley a book titled *A Great Run*, about the history of the hunt.

It was Sir Pat's love of hunting that enticed him to pursue a medical career. As a teenager he did not know what he was going to do with his life, although he was sure it would involve hunting. His father, a surgeon, pointed out that if he became a doctor he would have time to hunt on Tuesdays. 'So initially,' says Sir Pat, 'I studied medicine so I would have a profession that would allow me to hunt. However, I fell in love with medicine and I wanted to do something more demanding than general practice. So I specialised. And I found medicine even more exciting than hunting.'

Sir Pat's medical career led to several 'leading edge' developments in the hearing field, and much personal satisfaction in helping young children. He established the Deafness Research Foundation of New Zealand, which funded research in the field of hearing impairment. One of his studies investigated transplanting eardrums so that people who were lacking an eardrum, and therefore deaf, would be able to hear again.

Sir Patrick Eisdell Moore.

Simon Eisdell Moore leads the Pakuranga
Hunt field at Port Waikato.

Sir Patrick devoted a lot of time and energy to eradicating ear disease. Some very rewarding work took place on the East Coast of the North Island, where Sir Patrick attended a regular ear clinic at Te Puia Springs Hospital, north of Gisborne. One of his greatest thrills was seeing the delight on a child's face as they realised they could hear normally again.

Much of Sir Pat's work highlighted the importance of early intervention with hearing problems. He was instrumental in establishing the Hearing House, a centre that provides facilities, staff and expertise to give infants with hearing problems the intensive therapy and access to medical help they need. He was also involved with establishing mobile ear clinics that visit schools.

Sir Patrick had always thought that if he was ever given the choice between losing his sight or his hearing, he would chose the option of losing his sight. However, fate dealt a nasty hand, and over time both Sir Pat's sight and hearing have declined. Now he can only make out vague grey and black shadows, although he can read print with the help of a magnifying machine. He has completed an as yet unpublished manuscript of his life story, which is an absorbing and delightful tale written with humour and modesty.

Sir Pat's family connection with hunting continues. All four of his sons rode to hounds, and one son, Simon, who is crown solicitor for Auckland, is now deputy master of the Pakuranga Hunt. Now, in turn, Sir Pat's grandchildren are enjoying the thrill of hunting. The passion for horses, hunting and hounds continues down the generations, just as Sir Patrick gained his first experiences with his father. Long may the tradition continue.

RAY AND MARY COLES

EMERITUS MEMBERS OF THE NEW ZEALAND HUNTS' ASSOCIATION

IT IS RARE FOR A PROFESSIONAL HUNTSMAN to change roles and become the master of a hunt. In the history of New Zealand hunting there are few examples, but one is Ray Coles, retired huntsman of the Pakuranga Hunt, who went on to lead the field as master from 1985 to 1992. Ray and his wife Mary made a significant contribution to hunting in Pakuranga, and they remain interested and involved to this day through the deeds of their son Ross, who is the current huntsman.

Ray became a huntsman almost by default. When he returned from World War II and married Mary they decided to find a sharemilking position. However, despite searching widely, they could not locate a farm. At the time, the Pakuranga Hunt Committee was looking for a young huntsman to train to take over the role from long serving incumbent Val Smith. Pakuranga Hunt Committee member Cyril Fullerton encouraged Ray to apply, and he was successful, so beginning a five-year apprenticeship with Val that developed into a career as huntsman spanning the years from 1954 to 1982.

Ray stamped his mark on the breeding of the Pakuranga Hunt pack. He has a strong preference for tricoloured hounds, of the traditional harrier hound height, between 48.3 and 53.3 centimetres. The resulting pack became well matched in colour, height, conformation, temperament and ability, qualities that remain to this day.

Ray was also quick to make his mark on the traditional huntsman's role as clerk of the course at Ellerslie Racecourse. 'In the late 1950s I introduced the team of grey horses with riders in red

Ray Coles.

coats for the race meetings. It was a first in New Zealand and it is a spectacle that still stands.' One of the most memorable days was when eight greys and their riders paraded at the Royal Meet in 1954 when Queen Elizabeth II visited.

Mary was closely involved with the production of the first New Zealand Harrier Hound Studbook in 1988. The Studbook was produced on the initiative of then Christchurch Hunt Master Bruce Jessep after he returned from a hunting holiday in the United Kingdom. Ray was duly appointed secretary of the project; however, putting pen to paper has never been Ray's favourite pastime, so at his suggestion Mary was appointed in his place. Back then few hunts had comprehensive breeding records, and some huntsmen needed a lot of encouragement to put pen to paper. Mary had to establish a code system and sort through all the transfers of hounds that are made between packs, so the project was time-consuming. The resulting Studbook is a valued document that Phillip Langdale now produces annually at the completion of each season. The book includes contact details for the office holders of every hunt, a boundary map of the hunts, hound show results and other useful information.

In time, Ray and Mary's sons Graeme, Ross and Alan, went on to be whippers-in for their father. Graeme was enthusiastic to pursue a career as huntsman, but fate intervened and he was killed in a road accident in 1975, aged 23 years. Meanwhile, Ross was working for a meat-processing company. He, too, had been keen to become a huntsman, so it was Ross who took over the Pakuranga hounds on his father's retirement in 1982.

Ray's enthusiasm to follow hounds did not dim with his retirement as huntsman. It was a mark of respect for Ray when he was elected as master after Sir Patrick Eisdell Moore's retirement in 1984. When I asked Ray if it was difficult to change roles from huntsman to master, he replied, 'No, not really.' Then he laughed and added, 'Although when I was huntsman I only used to get into trouble with the hounds!'

Ray and Mary were elected as emeritus members of the New Zealand Hunts' Association in 1999 for their significant contribution to hunting in New Zealand. The emeritus membership is awarded infrequently as a mark of respect and honour to members who have provided long and distinguished service to New Zealand hunting.

At the end of the 1992 season Ray retired as master, but his enthusiasm for the sport and his love of people, horses and hunting remains. Together Ray and Mary have given so much to the sport of hunting in New Zealand. Their names are synonymous with hunting with the Pakuranga Hunt, and their legacy continues through their son Ross.

Barry Mansell

President of Manawatu Hunt

'There is nothing that can compare with riding a good horse following a pack of hounds in full cry with the wind whistling in your face,' says Barry Mansell, and there would be few people in New Zealand better qualified to comment. Barry has hunted since 1947, and over time has served as master, deputy master, president and whipper-in for the Manawatu Hunt and as chairman of the New Zealand Hunts' Association Harrier Hound Committee.

Hunting is an integral part of Barry's life and it is a sport that has brought him a lot of pleasure and good friends. When Barry talks about a good day's hunting the enthusiasm in his voice grows. 'I hunt for the thrill of the chase. When the hounds give tongue, its automatic that my horse and I are off to follow,' he says.

A person is always fortunate if his or her spouse enjoys the same sport, and Barry's wife Sue is an excellent rider who also loves hunting. 'When I met Sue,' Barry explains, 'I was involved with rugby. However, Sue was keen on hunting and that brought me back to the sport I had enjoyed as a child.' They married in 1961 and were made honorary life members of the Manawatu Hunt in 2001. Their children Penny and Tim both enjoyed hunting with their parents during their teenage years.

Both Barry and Sue have been prepared to give their time to support the sport they love. Both have been long-standing members of the Manawatu Hunt Committee, and Barry was joint master from 1971 to 1995, serving terms with the late Mrs June Johnston, Kevin Tweedie and Gary Freeman.

Sue Mansell ties husband Barry's stock.

Manawatu Huntsman Brian Clement (left), Manawatu President Barry Mansell (centre) and the Manawatu hounds (right) all take the fence in their own fashion.

Below: Manawatu Hunt Deputy Master John Proctor.

People remember Barry as an excellent master to follow. Manawatu Hunts-man Brian Clement says that when Barry was master, if a difficult fence came along, or some unclear boundaries, he would say, 'You can hunt anywhere with a bit of courage.'

Barry believes that a good master requires some experience working with hounds, and an understanding of how to make the field comfortable and produce good runs. 'A master needs good horses,' he says. 'And good interpersonal skills. He or she needs to remember that hunting should be fun, and at the same time preserve the traditions of hunting.'

In 1995, after 25 years of leading the field, Barry felt it was time for a change. 'There were good young deputy masters who were prepared to take on the job, and I thought the time was right for me to retire because if you stay too long you may lose some of the enthusiasm that makes for a good mastership.'

However, Barry was still keen to be involved with the hunt and was elected president in 1996. 'It was a role I sought, as I wanted to give something back to the sport I love,' he says. Sometimes masters retire because they are no longer comfortable jumping big fences, but this was definitely not so with Barry. From 1998 the opportunity arose to be whipper-in for Huntsman Brian Clement on a regular basis. It is a role that Barry loves. He relishes the challenge of being up

where the hounds work, which, along with Huntsman Brian Clement and fellow whipper-in David Liddle, means jumping whatever fences come his way.

When Barry is whipper-in he puts aside his president's role. 'When the hounds are being hunted, the huntsman has complete authority,' said Barry. 'Potentially, it could be delicate that I am the president, but Brian and I have a good relationship so there are no problems.' Barry knows all the hounds in the Manawatu pack by both name and pedigree. He is passionate about watching them work, is a decisive whipper-in, and a pleasure to watch in action.

The Manawatu Hunt was formed in 1910 and the committee is already preparing for the centenary celebrations in 2010. Whatever celebrations are planned will, no doubt, involve Barry and Sue. Deputy Master John Proctor summed it up when he said, 'Barry and Sue Mansell *are* the Manawatu Hunt. They have done more for the hunt then any other people I have ever known. They have been to the fore of the running of the hunt and their contribution has been unsurpassed. They don't come more dedicated or any better than Barry and Sue.'

Far right: Waikato Huntsman Lauryn Robertson
with the Waikato hounds at Te Akau beach.

DETAILS OF QUOTATIONS

Page 10
Sir Patrick Eisdell Moore
in *A Great Run* by P. W. Eisdell Moore and D. A. Bingley,
Tonson, Auckland, NZ, 1972, p122.

Page 30
Len McClelland
in *The Horse in New Zealand* by Elaine Power and Len McClelland,
Collins, Auckland and London, 1975, p48.

Page 52
Adrienne Taylor
Northland Hunt Jubilee Celebrations, April 2002.

Page 72
Ann Wilson
in *Gone Away, One hundred years with the Egmont-Wanganui Hunt Club*
by Laraine Sole, Egmont-Wanganui Hunt, Wanganui, NZ, p 25.

Page 83
Captain Douglas Bingley
in *A Great Run* by P. W. Eisdell Moore and D. A. Bingley,
Tonson, Auckland, NZ, 1972, p190.

Page 97
Duncan Holden
in *Harking Back II, A History of Hunting in New Zealand 1870–1989*
by Theo Herbert, Theo Herbert, Waipukurau, NZ, 1969, p.2.

Page 105
From *Weekly News*, Auckland, New Zealand, May 1874.

Page 116
Laraine Sole
in *Gone Away, One huntdred years with the Egmont-Wanganui Hunt Club* by Laraine Sole,
Egmont-Wanganui Hunt Club, Wanganui, NZ, p192.

Page 127
Duncan Holden in *Harking Back II, A History of Hunting in New Zealand 1870–1989*
by Theo Herbert, Waipukurau, NZ, 1969, p.3.

Page 132
Sir Patrick Eisdell Moore, Past Master Pakuranga Hunt, Past President NZHA, emeritus member NZHA.

Page 140
Sir Patrick Eisdell Moore
in *A Great Run*
by P. W. Eisdell Moore and D. A. Bingley, Tonson, Auckland, NZ, 1972, p6.

Cover image: Pakuranga Huntsman
Ross Coles leads the field home after
an autumn day's sport at Port Waikato
(also on pages 36,37).

Half title page: Northland Huntsman
Steve Clark.

Title pages: Property owner Robert
Richardson rides out with Waikato
Huntsman Lauryn Robertson at the
start of a meet at Te Akau.

Contents pages: On the property of
Pat Lowry, Immediate Past President
of the New Zealand Hunts Association.

First published in New Zealand in 2003 by
Tandem Press
PO Box 34 272
Birkenhead, Auckland
New Zealand
www.tandempress.co.nz

Copyright 2003
Text: Sarah Milne; photographs: Rob Tucker

Design and production:
Sally Hollis-McLeod, Moscow Design
Printed by Everbest Printing Ltd, China

NATIONAL LIBRARY OF NEW ZEALAND
CATALOGUING-IN-PUBLICATION DATA:
Milne, Sarah.
The thrill of the chase : celebrating hunting with harrier hounds in
New Zealand / Sarah Milne ; photographs by Rob Tucker.
ISBN 1-877298-10-7

1. Hunt riding—New Zealand.
2. Hare hunting—New Zealand.
3. Harrier (Dog breed) I. Tucker, Rob (Robert J.) II. Title.
799.230993—dc 21